A VIEW FOR FREEDOM

Alfie Roberts Speaks

on the Caribbean, Cricket, Montreal, and C.L.R. James

introduction by David Austin
afterword by Robert Hill

Alfie Roberts Institute 2005

1st edition, 1st printing
© Alfie Roberts Institute 2005
Foreword © David Austin
Afterword © Robert Hill

Printed in Canada

ISBN 0-9737178-0-7

Alfie Roberts Institute
5871 Victoria, Suite 220
Montreal, Quebec
H3W 2R7
Canada

Tel. 514-313-8938
Website: www.ari-iar.org

cover design by
James McGowan and David Austin

Acknowledgements

Several individuals made contributions towards the publication of this book. Since some of the contributors have asked to remain anonymous, we have maintained the anonymity of all financial contributors so as not to omit anyone. Please know that your contributions are genuinely appreciated and that this publication would not have happened without your generous support.

We would also like to send a special thank you to Jamie MGowan for laying out the publication and sharing with us his valuable insights on publishing. Last, thanks to Dwight Best for his assistance.

Alfie Roberts Institute

Table of Contents

A Brief Biography

Born in St. Vincent and the Grenadines on September 18, 1937 to Theodore and Naomi Roberts, Alfie Roberts attended St. George's Anglican School and then St. Vincent Boy's Grammar School in Kingstown. While at the Grammar School, Roberts excelled in both soccer and cricket and, upon the recommendation of cricket great Sir Everton Weekes, he was awarded a scholarship to Queen's Royal College in Trinidad where he shined as a cricketer before obtaining his Senior Cambridge School Certificate. It was during this period that he was selected to the West Indies cricket team. He toured New Zealand in 1955-56 and played his first and only test match. He was only 18 years of age, one of the youngest to ever play test cricket.

By 1961 Alfie Roberts was no longer playing competitive cricket. Between 1958 and 1962, he worked, like his father who was a government printer, as a civil servant for the government of St. Vincent. In 1962 he emigrated to Montreal, Canada to attend Sir George Williams (now Concordia) University. He graduated from Sir George with a degree in Political Science before pursuing and completing a graduate diploma in Public Administration at Carleton University in Ottawa. He worked as an administrator for Sidbec-Dosco, a steel company, for more than 25 years before retiring in 1993.

In 1965, Roberts teamed up with Robert Hill, Hugh O'Neale, Alvin Johnson, Franklyn Harvey, Ann Cools, and Rosie Douglas, among others, to organize the first of a series of conferences that would bring a host of distinguished Caribbean thinkers and writers to Montreal, including George Lamming and C.L.R. James. These events also nourished a host of new political movements across the Caribbean. Out of this group, the Conference Committee on West Indian Affairs, evolved several other groups based in Montreal, including the International Caribbean Service Bureau and the Emancipation 150 Committee. These groups were primarily concerned with social and political issues facing communities of Caribbean and African descent.

Among the many groups and organizations that Alfie Roberts helped to establish during his thirty-four years in Canada is the St. Vincent and Grenadines Association of Montreal. In fact, despite his many international commitments, he remained committed to his native St. Vincent and the Grenadines and it was he who, on the eve of the country's independence, submitted a detailed policy statement to the government of St. Vincent outlining why the Grenadines should be included as an integral part of the country's name. The crux of his argument was that the Grenadines should not be seen as mere appendages of the island of St. Vincent and that the integrity of all of the smaller islands should be respected. His submission was adopted by the government, hence the name St. Vincent and the Grenadines.

A voluminous reader who possessed a remarkably analytical mind, a vivid memory, and an insatiable appetite for learning, Alfie Roberts was also a teacher who served as an advisor and resource to many before his untimely death on July 24, 1996.

Within Us is Him

By Franklyn Harvey

He has said good-bye but he has
not left us,
Only the cosmic whole has gone
Holographs remain
With parts emphasized
In each of us

My most intellectually creative years were
with him
In this city of the two and many,
He is in me and I in him,
Part of me has gone to that other state
Part of him remains in who I am

In the heydays of the 60s
In the popular rebirthing of CLR James,
We were together with others
In helping to shape a great awakening
That touched many
Reverberating in the islands and the mainlands

He blew the horn of the forgotten
and the voiceless
For the little people, the creators of wealth
and culture,
For Everton Weekes, the forgotten "W" of
West Indian Cricket.

He was the keeper of the knowledge
The anchor of the principle
That every man, every woman, in every
place must be free
And, that when we move

we will say it's our natural freedom
that makes us move

He was the nurturer of the new initiates
He was the anchor,
The holder of the vision,
the keeper of the knowledge

The cosmic-human whole has left
But he is in us
We are in him

To Pat and the kids,
You have given much to us through Alfie
Know that we are here
As the many parts of him
To see you through

July 1996

Introduction

I myself feel I have done nothing. I lived the best way that I could and know how. I was always ready to listen and learn and to improve myself and to strive to improve, to know as much as is possible and feasible, always with the idea "If you know, teach; if you don't know, learn. Each one teach one." All this with a view for freedom.

Ideas can become important when they are taken hold of by many. They also need to become a material force. But how? That is the challenge for a better world today....

Great changes will take place in this part of the world, but not in our lifetimes. But change there will be as it took place in Egypt of antiquity, with the coming of Columbus, the American Revolution. The Russian Revolution, it has come and gone in front of our eyes. So while we do what we can, whether helping one here, helping one there, there is always this wider arena which can be influenced, however imperceptibly, by some organized activity.

— Alfie Roberts, July 1996

Ten years ago, almost to the day, I asked Alfie Roberts to participate in an interview. I was working on a magazine essay about events in Montreal in the 1960s and I wanted to capture his perspective on activities that he had been involved in during this period. Alfie agreed to what was supposed to be a short interview and we met on the evening of January 14, 1995. We gallivanted about the city for several hours, visiting bookstores and conversing with people whom we met along the way. By the time we sat down in the office of the Black Students' Network (BSN) at McGill University for the interview, it was already past 10 pm.

I had foolishly brought only two blank cassette tapes with me, one ninety minutes in length and another of sixty minutes. Given the usual length of my conversations with Alfie (they often lasted several

11

hours and, during one phone conversation, I watched the sun set and rise as we spoke) I should have known better. We left the BSN office at approximately 2 am. Fortunately, I happened to have in my possession another cassette that already had material recorded on it—a lecture by the renowned political scientist, Ali Mazrui—which I was then forced to record over. It is in part thanks to Ali Mazrui that this publication exists in its current form.

In the interview, Alfie not only talk about Montreal in the 1960s and the now infamous Sir George Williams Incident at what is today Concordia University.[1] Long before we reached "the main point" of the interview, Alfie delved into the details of his own political evolution, going back to his childhood in St. Vincent and the Grenadines, his relatively short cricket career (this he did reluctantly[2]), as well as the work of the Montreal-based Conference Committee on West Indian Affairs and his association with C.L.R. James. The result of the unexpectedly long interview is a rare and unusual glimpse into the inner thinking of a remarkably analytical mind.

Regrettably, as fate would have it, and much to the surprise of

[1] The Sir George Williams Affair was a watershed incident in the development of Montreal's Black community and had a profound effect on both the Canadian and Caribbean socio-political landscapes. There were protests throughout the Caribbean in support of the West Indian students on trial in Montreal. The largest of these protests took place in Trinidad, sparked in part by a visit to the University of the West Indies by Daniel Roland Michener, the Canadian Governor-General, in what appeared to be an attempt to do damage control on the heels of the arrests of the students at Sir George. Students came out in droves to protest the Governor General's visit, forcing him to leave the university campus. These demonstrations became widespread and more generalized, led by Geddes Granger of the National Joint Action Committee (NJAC) and George Weekes of the Oilfield Workers Trade Union. The mass protests brought the country to a standstill and almost led to the overthrow of the Eric Williams government in 1970 (Ivar Oxaal, *Race and Revolutionary Consciousness: A Documentary Interpretation of the 1970 Black Power Revolt in Trinidad* [Cambridge, Mass.: Schenkman Publishing Company, Inc., 1968) and Selwyn Ryan and Taimoon Stewart, *The Black Power Revolution 1970: A Retrospective* [St. Augustine: University of the West Indies, 1995]). For an in-depth analysis of the Sir George Williams Affair and its implications for Canada and the Caribbean, see Dennis Forsythe, ed., *Let the Niggers Burn: The Sir George Williams University Affair and its Caribbean Aftermath* (Montreal: Black Rose-Our Generation Press, 1971). For a more journalistic account of the events of 1969 in Montreal, see Dorothy Eber's *The Computer Centre Party: Canada Meets Black Power. That Sir George Williams Affair* (Montreal: Tundra Books of Montreal, 1969).

[2] It has never been entirely clear why Roberts decided to hang up his cricket bat. He did, however, drop a hint. On the 1956 tour to New Zealand, Roberts witnessed an incident that, for him, signified all that was wrong with the West Indies cricket at the time. Weekes was up to bat and his partner, having already earned his century, appeared to deliberately allow himself to be

all who knew him, Alfie Roberts passed away on July 24, 1996, only eighteen months after we sat down for what, in light of his death, has now become a historic interview. As a result, the narrative below represents the most extensive autobiographical and political account that he left behind. Since my own relationship with Alfie Roberts was as much a personal one as it was political, at the risk of being overly self-indulgent, I would like to talk a bit about my earliest encounter with him and the impact that he had on me as an individual.

I first met Alfonso Theodore Roberts, simply known to his friends as Alfie, in January 1991. I had just moved to Montreal after eight youthful years in Toronto and I was anxious to meet people who were politically active in the city. During a visit to the now defunct Liberation Books that was located in the downtown core of Montreal, I discovered an organization called *Also Known as X* (AKAX), a group of young Black women and men who, in addition to organizing against the brutality and shootings of young Blacks by Montreal police officers, facilitated weekly "rap sessions" at which guests were invited to speak on a wide array of social, political and cultural issues. It was at one of these AKAX sessions at Concordia University that I first met Alfie.

Alfie was the guest speaker that night and his talk immediately struck a chord with me. I had migrated to Montreal, largely because I felt the need to develop and evolve politically. As a high school student, I, along with a number of other young women and men, would meet on Saturdays at the legendary Third World Books on Bathurst Street in Toronto for weekly discussions on historical, cultural and political issues. Many of us would read books during the week, anxiously anticipating those informal weekend sessions. We often exchanged information—audio and videotapes, documents and books—mostly, though not exclusively, dealing with issues related to

bowled out so as to prevent Weekes from earning a century of his own. In a public discussion in 1997 in Montreal, Weekes confirmed the story but would not name who his batting partner was. In the same meeting Weekes, once a mentor to Roberts, stated that even at the early age of 18 Roberts seemed more bent towards politics and bringing about change in his native St. Vincent and throughout the world than making a career out of cricket. Roberts often recounted that during the West Indian tour of New Zealand in 1956 he witnessed a number of incidents that irked him. One was that the "small island" players were treated differently than players from the larger islands. He also noted that those players with a limited education were treated as lesser people. As Weekes also attests, Roberts could not understand why the captain of the West Indies team was traditionally White, despite the presence of such great players as Weekes, Clyde Walcott, and Frank Worrell.

Africa and the Caribbean. We also studied aspects of African-American history though, tellingly, Canadian, including African-Canadian history, was not a significant part of our agenda at the time. Many of us were particularly enamoured with Malcolm X and we would debate the merits of violent versus non-violent action with a sense of urgency—as if the issue had direct bearing on our own lives, which in fact it did. It was our man Malcolm against Martin Luther King. In those days we were a long way from recognizing the revolutionary role that King had played in his effort to liberate the United States from itself. Few of us had heard his resounding, indicting and, ultimately compelling condemnation of the war in Vietnam and the scurrilous machinations of the Cold War—a speech that many believe underscored the need to elimate him by those bent on silencing him. In those headstrong days, some of us, quite scandalously, went as far as calling Dr. King "Martin Luther Coon". We had much to learn.

At Third World Books, under the watchful eye of Lennie, as we affectionately called Mr. Leonard Johnson, who along with his wife, Mrs. Gwendolyn Johnson, ran the store, I was exposed to a wide range of literature on and by African and Caribbean peoples and about global politics and economics. Lennie would suggest reading C.L.R. James's *The Black Jacobins*, Walter Rodney's *Groundings with My Brothers* and *How Europe Underdeveloped Africa*, Frantz Fanon's *The Wretched of the Earth* and *Black Skin, White Masks*, and various Socialist texts—all of which I did read but, I must confess, did not, could not, fully grasp at the time. This was the late 1980s at the height of what can be seen as the resurrection of Negritude and Black Power, a time in which we zealously sought to reclaim and appropriate our African ancestry. We also read Cheikh Anta Diop's classic work *The African Origins of Civilization: Myth or Reality*; Ivan Van Sertima's seminal work, *They Came Before Columbus*, which explored the pre-Columbian presence of Africans in the Americas, and various writings by authors such as Dr. John Henrik Clarke and Yosef Ben-Jochanon on ancient and modern African history. Our bias in favour of male authors is obvious in hindsight, but we were also exposed to the writings of Audre Lorde, bell hooks, and Angela Davis. Those were heady, exciting days and many of us came of age in that bookstore.

These earlier experiences at Third World Books left an indelible mark on me; yet by the time I finished high school and was thinking about my next move, I was beginning to feel as though my development was being arrested. Our discussions at the bookstore became increasingly circular and were not attached to any organized grouping or movement. I began to feel restless and was seriously considering leaving the city. Montreal seemed a logical site of relocation. As a child, I had spent two years in Montreal before moving to Toronto in 1982 and I had fond memories of the city. Furthermore, in reading Walter Rodney's *Grounding with My Brothers* (three of the lectures presented in this popular book were delivered in Montreal) and a book edited by Denis Forsythe entitled *Let the Niggers Burn!*—a book about the Sir George Williams student protest in 1969 that my older brother, Andrew, had pointed out to me when I was in high school—I discovered that Montreal had been the site of some important, indeed historic developments related to North America and the Caribbean. Much of this history is described by Alfie Roberts below.

I returned to Montreal determined to discover what had made the city a locus of expatriate Caribbean and Black activity from the 1960s through the 1980s, and the catalyst for a number of historically important turning points in Caribbean, North American, and by extension, world history. Meeting Alfie was an important part of this quest and, as we shall see in his narrative below, Alfie was not solely a troubadour who clarified and passed on this history to succeeding generations; he had been a living, breathing part of it.

Alfie lived and embodied the very experience that I was intent on unearthing, a political tradition that he constantly sought to commit to our collective consciousness. He had been a young cricketer for the West Indies, anointed along with a young Gary Sobers by none other than cricket great Sir Everton Weekes. As a tireless ambassador of his people, he travelled widely and was associated with C.L.R. James, Walter Rodney, and a number of other luminaries within the Pan-African political tradition. And he spread the gospel, hoping that the next generation would continue the struggle for a more just and humane world, a struggle of which he and his fellow travellers had been an integral part.

Although I sat in admiration of the depth and breadth of Aflie's talk during the AKAX session—his sweeping, yet tempered, poignant remarks, punctuated by one historical insight or another—to this day, I cannot remember the actual subject matter of the lecture delivered that cold Friday winter evening. But there is one particular part of his talk that left its imprint. At some point, his panoramic address centred on the political scene in Canada and the divergent political approaches of then prime minister, Brian Mulroney, and the former prime minister, Pierre Elliot Trudeau. In reflecting on their respective tenures in office, Alfie described the social background of each individual and the way in which their personal upbringings had shaped their political outlooks and behaviour patterns. For Alfie, Mulroney's humble roots and his hard-nosed rise to power meant that he consistently felt the need to prove himself and to seek affirmation from the more established elite and wealthy in Canada and the United States. His conservative economic and political policies, not to mention what some would describe as his almost sycophantic admiration for U.S. president Ronald Reagan and his close relationship with British prime minister Margaret Thatcher, could at least be partially traced back to his upbringing and class background as a child.

Trudeau, was of a different ilk. Born into big money and, as a result, never having been at the vagaries of anybody, he exuded a genuine air of confidence and defiance. Despite his popularity and his playful antics, he often presented a somewhat imperious, at times dismissive "just watch me" attitude that was rarely censored. And in the heat of the Cold War, his confident independent spirit permitted him to normalize relations between Canada and Cuba and even to develop a personal friendship with Fidel Castro, despite sometimes vigorous protests from the United States. Trudeau's supreme confidence and his disregard for protocol also permitted him, according to the legend, to hurl an expletive at a political opponent in Canada's House of Commons, an act for which, if the legend is correct, he also unequivocally refused to apologize.[3]

By mapping the differences between the two prime ministers, Alfie was insisting that in order to understand what motivates individuals, in this case politicians, we have to situate them and their actions within the context of their personal histories. In contrast to those social critics and political theorists who get so carried away with grand schemes and narratives that they often fail to see what is most obvious, even when it sits right beneath their very noses, Alfie

---

[3] Alfie Roberts met Trudeau on at least one occasion when Trudeau was in office. As the story goes, Trudeau was so impressed with Roberts insights that he hinted at further meetings to which Alfie ever-so-subtly discouraged and ultimately declined. He was never very comfortable with, or perhaps more precisely, never permitted himself to get too close to power.

insisted on this form of psycho-social historical analysis as a determinant—though certainly not the only one—in understanding the roles that individuals assume in the arena of politics. He always sought to discover the personal circumstances that impinged on the lives of people and that helped to shape the actions that they would take. As a result, he was very sensitive to the aims and motivations, strengths and weaknesses of collaborators and foes and was rarely caught by surprise by some errant or wayward act.

Alfie had an impressive library. He possessed thousands of books which, at the time of his death, were littered all over his home. As Phil Jenkins of the *Ottawa Citizen* wrote shortly after Alfie died, his library was "a unique storehouse of the history of dignity in the face of oppression". He was a bibliophile who read voluminously. His late wife Pat, herself an avid reader who was very actively involved in Montreal's Black community, maintained that Alfie read almost all of the thousands of books that he possessed. (Pat herself read a fair number of them too).

I have a vivid memory of Alfie turning to me on one occasion and stating: "Dave, I have come to the conclusion that I cannot read everything," a thought that he uttered with a good deal of lament, as if he had once genuinely believed that he indeed could read everything. But Alfie did not simply read books. Nor was he an empty vessel that simply retained and internalised what his eyes absorbed. He was blessed with a remarkable ability to synthesize material with his own complex thoughts and he remains among the most sophisticated thinkers that I have encountered. And, as Jenkins argues, for Alfie, books "were not sacred; Alfie didn't collect books in order to sit in the midst of their unused perfection. They were the means to the end of becoming masters of ourselves, something he believed, the way priests believe, we all should become."

Alfie read voluminously and was particularly well versed in the history and politics of the Caribbean, Africa, and the Soviet Union. He was also an acute student of Marxist theory. I once saw him outclass a somewhat arrogant professor of Russian history who, when he finally finished pronouncing and permitted Alfie to speak, was bedazzled by Alfie's detailed, comprehensive analysis of the Russian Revolution. In fact, the professor felt compelled to, diplomatically, ask Alfie just how he knew so much (read: *how did this non-academic Black man know so much*) about Soviet history, as he ever so subtly implored Alfie to assist him in his research.

An avid listener and follower of jazz music, Alfie possessed an elaborate jazz collection and was constantly exploring this art form. Once on a radio program, he was asked to comment on a speech by Marcus Garvey. He proceeded to situate the tenor and cadence of Garvey's elocution within the rhythm and tempo of some of the great jazz tunes of Garvey's era. It was a relationship that I had never heard anyone contemplate and I listened in amazement.

Despite his vivid memory and the assiduous attention he paid to detail, Alfie was distinguished because of his remarkable ability to cut through morass and confusion and get to the heart of an issue. This ability stemmed from another gift—Alfie was incredibly perceptive. In talking with him, one had the distinct impression that behind every action, phenomenon, or physical entity, there was a story to know and lessons to be learned, and that he was constantly and painstakingly working to uncover that story. His eyes honed in on what most did not see and he was always simultaneously trying to think both behind and ahead; drawing lessons from the past in order to inform his, and consequently our, understanding of the present and the future. He strove to assess nothing at face value and took nothing for granted.

As an example, I remember Alfie recounting a story about how, as a young boy in St. Vincent and the Grenadines, he would tidy his room and arrange his shoes in the closet, only to realize that he would have to go through the same motions the next day, rearranging his shoes, closet, and room, in an effort to restore it to its previous order. What this taught this precocious child was that the only thing constant in life is change and that order is often derived from chaos. It was lessons like these that this prococious boy would carry with him as he matured into adulthood and travelled to various parts of the world. These intuitive insights would later be buttressed by elaborate reading and investigation. But the core of his person was there at a very early age.

Alfie was about people and was always for the underdog. As a result, he neither tired of stressing both the positive attributes and shortcomings that characterized various societies. His observations of the many countries that he visited are telling. In Ghana, for example, he was alarmed at the sight of the personal drivers of the Ghanaian elite walking miles at night along long dusty roads to their own homes after depositing their employers at their doorsteps. In Libya he cringed at the way in which Libyan authorities barked orders at civilians. He would then contrast those observations with his experience in Tanzania while attending the Sixth Pan-African Congress in 1974. Having visited New Zealand, Europe, Russia, Ghana, Uganda, Libya, Martinique and most of the Anglophone Caribbean; living in Canada and having spent a good deal of time in the United States, he consistently described Tanzania as one of the only countries where people could communicate with and talk back to police officers and authorities without fear of reprisal. For Alfie, this was a significant barometer of social development in that country.

The concern here is not whether his observations are a hundred percent accurate. Undoubtedly, as I am certain Alfie would admit, notwithstanding the Anglophone Caribbean which he was intimately familiar with, his relatively brief visits to various countries obviously limited the extent to which he could observe and understand those societies in great depth. Certainly, his observations provide insight, not only into those societies as he observed them, but into the way his mind worked. He was always examining and exploring the social relations between people, the relationships between classes and, more specifically, the way in which the underprivileged and marginalized were treated by authority and the well-to-do. And from his early days as a first class, indeed world class, cricketer, up until his waning days when he was gripped with illness, Alfie was constantly assessing and drawing conclusions which he used as a ruler to measure the extent to which a society was developing and the possibilities that a given society augured for a better tomorrow.

With time and reflection, Alfie Roberts has come to represent many things for me. Increasingly, I find myself comparing him to another Caribbean national and Pan-African figure who, despite his stature, has yet to receive the serious attention that he deserves. I have in mind here George Padmore, that remarkable individual from Trinidad whose work in England in the 1930s through to the 1950s played a pivotal role in the independence movements that swept the African continent in the 1950s and 1960s. It is said of Padmore that no one concerned with African emancipation passed through London without coming into contact with him. His influence stretched far and wide and he worked alongside a whole generation of Africans and West Indians who would go on to play prominent roles in the independence movements of their native countries, including Kwame Nkrumah of Ghana, Nnamdi Azikiwe of Nigeria, Jomo Kenyatta of Kenya, and Eric Williams of Trinidad.[4]

I have come to see Alfie as a kind of Padmore who, despite his many roles, worked to achieve for the Caribbean what Padmore worked so tirelessly to accomplish in Africa. In the 1960s and 1970s, the Roberts' apartment on Bedford Street in the Cote-des-Neiges district of Montreal was a political stomping ground where books could be borrowed by friends, Caribbean students, political activists, and aspiring politicians. It was a place where dusk till dawn discussions were held on a wide array of subjects, and where political strategies were mapped out. Alfie and his wife Patricia hosted many sessions in their Montreal home, earning it the name "The University of Bedford," and many people, including several future Caribbean prime ministers, came of age politically in their living room.

But the story does not end in the Montreal apartment. Alfie and his cohorts helped to catalyse into existence the Anglophone Caribbean's New Left in the 1960s and 1970s. The Conference Committee on West Indian Affairs (CCWIA)—a group that included Alfie Roberts, Alvin Johnson, Hugh O'Neale, Robert Hill, Gloria Simmons, Franklyn Harvey, Ann Cools, Bridget Joseph, Jean Depradine, Tim Hector, Rosie Douglas, among others—was instrumental in this process. This group helped to recreate the Caribbean in microcosm in Montreal and, in the process, helped to

---

[4] George Padmore was C.L.R. James' boyhood friend from Trinidad. Padmore became an active member of the Communist Party while studying in the United States and eventually left for the Soviet Union to continue his political work. He became the head of the Red International Labour Union's Negro Bureau and worked tirelessly for the cause of Black liberation and African emancipation with the backing and resources of the Soviet Union. He even served as a member of the Moscow city soviet (the equivalent of a city council) for a brief period. Among Padmore's publications during this period include: *The Life and Struggle of Negro Toilers; What is the International Trade Union Committee of Negro Workers?; Negro Workers and the Imperialist War; Forced Labour in Africa; American Imperialism Enslaves Liberia;* and *Labour, Imperialism and East Africa.* Padmore split from the Soviet Union in 1933 after being asked by his superiors to temper his anti-colonial activities targeting France and Britain as these two countries and the Soviet Union sought to normalize relations in the interest of fighting fascism. Padmore founded the International African Service Bureau (IASB) in England in the mid-1930s with C.L.R. James as the editor of the organization's newspaper, the *International African Opinion.* His post-Soviet publications include: *How Britain Rules Africa* (1936), *Africa and World Peace* (1937), *How Russia Transformed Her Colonial Empire* (1946), *Africa: Britain's Third Empire* (1949), *The Gold Coast Revolution* (1953) and perhaps his most well-known book, *Pan Africanism or Communism?* (1956). Other members of the IASB included Ras Makonnen, Jomo Kenyatta and Amy Ashwood Garvey. Kwame Nkrumah would also join Padmore in England and together they organized the historic 1945 Fifth Pan-African Congress in Manchester, England, a meeting that has been credited for laying the theoretical foundation for the African independence movement. Padmore went on to join Kwame Nkrumah in the newly-independent Ghana as an advisor where he passed away in 1959. For more on the life of Padmore, see James R. Hooker, *Black revolutionary: George Padmore's path from communism to pan-Africanism* (New York: Praeger, 1967); and Bill Schwarz, "George Padmore," in *West Indian Intellectuals in Britain,* ed. by Bill Schwarz (Manchester, UK: Manchester University Press, 2003).

humanize the existence of Blacks in Canada and members of the wider society. And yet it is worth noting that Hill, Harvey, Hector, and Douglas all became significant political figures in their respective countries.

Hill was with Abeng in Jamaica following the 1968 Rodney Riots when Walter Rodney was expelled from Jamaica after participating in the historic Congress of Black Writers in Montreal. Harvey was with the New Beginning Movement and later with the Movement for Assemblies of People, which evolved into the New Jewel Movement in Grenada and ushered in the Grenada Revolution. Hector founded the Antigua Caribbean Liberation Movement; while Douglas, was somewhat of a roving ambassador who would later become prime minister of his native Dominica.[5]

Alfie remained in Montreal and was a co-founder of the International Caribbean Service Bureau (ICSB), which evolved out of the CCWIA and included Allan Brown, Barry Burgher, Viola Daniel,

---

[5] Apart from Hugh O'Neale and *Montreal Star* journalist Alvin Johnson who died in a car accident in 1966, the core members of the Conference Committee on West Indian Affairs went on to pursue some very significant work. Robert Hill returned to Jamaica where he continued his studies and became ensconced in the political struggles that ensued after the banning of Walter Rodney from Jamaica in 1968. His work was primarily centred around the group *Abeng*, which emerged on the heels of Walter Rodney being banned from Jamaica by the Shearer government in October 1968. Hill served as the editor of *Abeng's* weekly organ of the same name. Today he is a renowned professor of history at UCLA, an authority on Marcus Garvey and the UNIA, and Rastafari. He is also the Literary Executor of the C.L.R James Estate. The late Leonard Tim Hector returned to his native Antigua and Barbuda where he became an important political figure within the Caribbean left. He also sat in the Antiguan senate and was the publisher of the leading opposition paper, the *Outlet,* in which he penned his sweeping "Fan the Flame" essays. A disciple of C.L.R. James, he also served on the West Indies Cricket Board and became an important Pan-African figure throughout the Caribbean. Franklyn Harvey left Montreal for Trinidad and was one of the founding members of the popular-based, bottom up, New Beginning Movement. He was later a founder of the Movement for Assemblies of People (MAP) in Grenada, a grouping that eventually merged with JEWEL to form the New Jewel Movement and usher in the Grenada Revolution. Today he lives in Ottawa but remains very much involved in international development work and nurturing new leadership. The late Rosie Douglas was one of the key organizers of the 1968 Congress of Black Writers and both Douglas and Ann Cools were active in the 1969 Sir George Williams University Affair for which they were jailed. Before becoming prime minister of Dominica, Douglas was well known for his active involvement in African and Caribbean affairs. He has been credited for playing a role in galvanizing support for the African National Congress, particularly crucial Libyan support, during apartheid. Ann Cools became very active in the women's movement in the 1960s and 1970s and is credited with founding one of the first women's shelters in Canada. Today she is a senator, Canada's first Black woman in that position. Gloria Simmons was the secretary of the Conference Committee on West Indian Affairs and Jean Depradine also played an important organizational role within the group, as did Bridget Joseph. In fact, the 1967-68 *Caribbean Conference Bulletin* published by the Conference Committee pays tribute to Ann Cools (Barbados), Bridget Joseph (Grenada), Gloria Simmons (Bermuda) and Jean Depradine (Barbados), describing them as "the living indication that the Caribbean woman will be in the forefront of the movement for a new Caribbean."

and Ede Howell.[6] He later co-founded the Emancipation 150 Committee. Both organizations issued statements, organized fora and other public events, and carried out educational activities which sensitised the wider public to developments in both the Caribbean and Africa while galvanizing support for various political movements.

It is hardly a coincidence that the ICSB is almost identical in name to the International African Service Bureau in which Padmore played a leading role. Alfie and his co-conspirators were consciously walking in the footsteps of Padmore, C.L.R. James, Claudia Jones, and a host of Caribbean and Pan-African figures who struggled to humanize their existence and to make the world a more sane and inhabitable place.

Unlike Padmore, who eventually moved to Ghana to continue his work on the African continent, Alfie did not return to the Caribbean to live and pursue the work that he began abroad. But the opportunities were not lacking. When a group of Caribbean political figures were beginning to think through the possibility of establishing a Pan-Caribbean organization in the Caribbean, Alfie was the individual to whom they turned to play a, if not the, leading role. And when the time appeared ripe to create such an organization in Grenada during the Grenada Revolution, Alfie's late wife, Patricia, assured me that a Cuban representative and Maurice Bishop, then prime minister of Grenada, called Alfie on several occasions requesting that he come to Grenada and "make his contribution". This should come as no surprise. Alfie knew Bishop and other leaders of the Grenada Revolution well (Bishop had been a guest of the ICSB in Montreal in 1975). Curiously, Alfie declined the invitation to Grenada. There are perhaps many reasons for this but it has been suggested that he was aware of the internal political dynamics in Grenada that would eventually lead to its malaise. As a non-Grenadian (though his mother was originally from Grenada), and ever-conscious of the reality of perception, he was likely reluctant to enter a situation that might be plagued with uncertainty in a country in which he might be looked upon as an interfering foreigner.

---

[6] Alternatively known as the Caribbean International Service Bureau, the ICSB issued policy statements, drafted numerous letters, and organized fora and conferences on the Caribbean which brought together a number of leading figures from the Caribbean's Left, including Maurice Bishop, Richard Hart, C.L.R. James, Trevor Munroe, and Walter Rodney.

Whatever his reasons, Alfie remained in Montreal and it is left to our imaginations to envisage what might have been. Somewhat later in life, when several individuals with whom he had been closely associated in Montreal were on the threshold of political office in the Caribbean, Alfie contemplated the prospect of returning to the region to work in whatever capacity he might be useful. Having retired after more than 25 years of service at his full-time job, he was ready to embark upon a new stage in his life. It was precisely at this point that his life was cut short.

When a proper history of Canada's connection to the Caribbean is written, the role that the West Indian-Canadian community has played in shaping the modern Caribbean will have to be seriously considered. Montreal will have a special place in this history and the results will be quite a revelation to many. This is part of the story I was searching for when I arrived in Montreal and stumbled upon Alfie. But there is certainly no need to stop at the Caribbean or with African-Canadians when describing the scope of Alfie's influence. There are numerous continental Africans who, to this day, see him as a guiding light in their social and political awakening. Alfie was as much dedicated to genuine African liberation as he was to the struggle for justice and freedom for Caribbean and Black people in general. He was about liberation and justice for all and, to that end, he also worked with individuals of diverse ethnic and social backgrounds—union workers, politicians, intellectuals, activists, etc., from across the globe.

C.L.R. James had a deep respect and admiration for Alfie. Once, in responding to a question from a friend of Alfie's, James was informed of Alfie's opinion on that question, and James is then reported to have said, "Well, if Alfie said it is so, then it must be so." With his great intellect and wide study, Alfie could have easily been a university professor as a number of his associates and friends had become. Yet he chose a different route, a direction that embodied Marx's maxim that "philosophers have interpreted the world in various ways...the point is to change it." I am not trying to create what would be a false dichotomy between academia and working for social change. I simply would like to make the point that Alfie lived for change and organized his life accordingly. Fascinated with working class life, he worked in the administration department of a steel company upon completing his graduate studies in Public Administration at Carleton University.

I can recall with great humour one occasion in 1994 when Alfie Roberts and I, along with a professor friend, met with the legendary Egyptian economist, Samir Amin, who was visiting Montreal on a lecture tour. The professor introduced herself to Amin and described her research interests and I introduced myself as a journalist (I was interviewing him for an article I planned to write). When it was Alfie's turn, he simply said: "Alfie Roberts. I'm in steel." I was supposed to be interviewing Amin solo so it is quite possible that he was genuinely confused about the two additional guests. But the awkward silence and the puzzled look on his face following Alfie's introduction however, seemed to suggest that he was pondering how this "man of steel" had arrived in his midst.

But Alfie was very proud that he worked in the steel industry. Some years after, when he had retired from his full-time job, I asked him about the nature of his work and he proudly described how much he had enjoyed working at the heart of Quebec's steel industry where he could observe working class life. This was no voyeuristic adventurism on his part. The details of his work at Sidbec-Dosco steel plant are still somewhat foggy, but it appears that he was involved in union activity at the plant. Since the 1960s, he had been a student of the theories of Karl Marx and working class history. Working in a steel plant, he was consciously marrying his theoretical and historical education with practical experience in the labour force. This was part of his life-long effort to better understand the world in which we live and how to change it for the better.

How is it that, aside from those who had direct contact with him, so few people know about Alfie Roberts' social and political contributions? Part of the answer lies in the fact that, even in death, his life is symbolic of the work that is yet to be done. As he states below, one of his motivations for leaving St. Vincent and the Grenadines in 1962 for Montreal was to discover the role that Africans and their descendents had played in history. He wasted no time embarking upon this mission once he stepped foot in North America. I would like to make the point here that some forty years after he embarked on his eternal quest for knowledge, there still remains a tremendous amount of history, sitting right under our very noses, that we have yet to excavate, chronicle, and embrace. This is dead history, or at least dead to our consciousness, that needs to be resurrected, history from which we can glean those ever-important lessons for the present and the future. In his own efforts to uncover this history for himself, Alfie became a historical figure in his own right, one who personifies much of what his brand of "archaeological" work revealed.

As we struggle to create a more just, equitable, and humane world—a prospect for which Alfie, the consummate optimist, never doubted possible—we need to exhume and bring to life this dormant history and, in uncovering it, live up to a responsibility that Alfie and so many others have bequeathed us. In today's tumultuous times, as we struggle to preserve our humanity and reward the inestimable sacrifices that our forebears have made, it falls upon us to assume the responsibility of building the kind of world that we would like to see in the here and now. Of course, this is a task that, with all of its challenges and obstacles, Alfie embraced with open arms. He understood that change does not fall from the sky or occur as a result of thunderous social eruptions—though eruptions of this kind certainly have, and can, contribute to change. He genuinely believed that we—you and I—make change and he never failed to draw on historical examples of human beings *making history*, examples which demonstrate that, even when, or at times because, our backs are straightened to the wall and all appears to be lost, we find the resolve to create change.

David Austin
Montreal, Canada
January 12, 2005

Alfie Roberts Speaks

Editorial Note

Alfie Roberts was a great storyteller and, in editing the text, every effort has been made not to disrupt the flow of his narrative. The questions that were posed to him, having served their purpose during the interview, have been eliminated from the text altogether.

The order of the narrative differs from that of the original interview in some instances. These adjustments were made in order to group certain ideas and, when appropriate, place them in historical sequence. When necessary, tenses have been changed, sentences rearranged, and words eliminated in order to avoid unnecessary repetition. Every effort was made to respect the integrity of his thoughts and his unique speaking style.

In a sense, this text represents the last testament of Alphonso Theodore Roberts. So little has been written about him and the work in which he was involved. Due to this—coupled with the fact that he did not live to edit the interview himself, suggest changes, or clarify any of his remarks—extensive footnotes have been added. Additional footnotes reflect a commitment to making the text as accessible as possible to a wide cross-section of people, including a younger readership that may not be familiar with many of the references that are mentioned throughout.

Several individuals made comments on the text or assisted in the editing at various stages in this book's development. Special thanks to Bathseba Belai, Nantali Indongo, Pat Harewood, Celia Daniel, Adrian Harewood, and Robert Hill.

David Austin

A View for Freedom: Alfie Roberts Speaks

The Early Days

I came to Montreal in 1962. The West Indian Federation[1] had already come into being and broke up, rightly so I thought because it was a bastardized federation; it wasn't an independent federation. It was a federation made up of colonial countries. So when there was a referendum in Jamaica as to whether or not Jamaica should continue in the federation, and the population in Jamaica voted against it— when there was consternation in many spheres about "the break-away federation"—I didn't see anything wrong with that. I thought it was a good thing because the federation rested on a colonial basis and I thought the islands should have been independent, that federation should have rested on a more independent basis. That was my way of thinking concerning the Federation.

Even prior to the Federation, I lived through a period in St. Vincent and the Grenadines when there was a divide between one era and another. Adult franchise, "one person, one vote," came into being in 1951. Up to 1951 you were only able to vote if you had access to property and a certain monetary income. But in 1951 adult franchise came into being, especially based on the work of a man called George McIntosh, the grandfather of Julian McIntosh who is around here with us.[2] And he was an ardent federationist. He was a man who had agitated in the thirties. As a matter of fact, he was the only person, as far as I can think of, who was tried for treason in the whole colonial and British Empire, whether it's in Africa or Asia. Sixty years ago McIntosh was adjudged to be one of the leading personalities in fomenting that disturbance and he was tried for treason during what was called a "riot" in St. Vincent and the Grenadines, part of the turbulent thirties in the English-speaking Caribbean (he won the case). So he was one of the leading lights of the time, a man who was agitating. He fought for the rights of the Shaker, akin to the

---

[1] For a detailed account of the rise and fall of the West Indian Federation see F.A. Hoyos, *Grantley Adams and the Social Revolution* (London and Basingstoke: Macmillan, 1974) and C.L.R. James, *Federation: "We Failed Miserably", How and Why* (San Juan: Vedic Enterprises Ltd., 1962).

[2] Julian McIntosh is a versatile musician and music instructor and an active member of Montreal's Black community.

Pocomania[3] people in Jamaica. He talked about land reform and a lot of those social and economic issues pertinent to the down-pressed of society and was one of the people agitating for "one person, one vote," adult franchise which came into being in 1951.

McIntosh was away in England on a convention arranged by the British government when "one person, one vote" was being introduced. What one can see in retrospect is that the British authorities probably kept him outside the country in order to diminish his influence in terms of agitating around elections. But like everything else, those people miscalculated because there is always gestation in the innards of society. And what happened is that prior to the elections, in the autumn of 1951, a man called Ebenezer Theodore Joshua arrived in St. Vincent and the Grenadines from Trinidad and Tobago. He was originally from St. Vincent and the Grenadines but had gone to Trinidad and became one of the top personalities inside of the British Empire Workers and Citizens Home Rule Party led by a man called Tubal Uriah "Buzz" Butler.[4]

In reading the paper put out by this political grouping led by Butler, Joshua, who at the time was a school master, would point out the typographical errors in the paper and, by virtue of that, was recruited to look over the paper before it was published. So he clandestinely began his association with Butler's party and eventually I think he went full-time into that party and rose right to the top of the party.

Then another man by the name of George Charles who was also in Trinidad (at a later period to Joshua but also affiliated with the Butler party) arrived in St. Vincent. And these individuals got together with some others and they formed what you call The Eighth Army. This group of eight people—there were eight constituencies at

[3] The Shaker movement in St. Vincent and the Pocomania movement in Jamaica are variants of a number of Afro-Christian syncretic religious movements that emerged throughout the Caribbean following the slavery. Slaves were not permitted to openly practice their African religious beliefs for fear that they would translate into rebellion. For the Shaker movement in St. Vincent, see Wallace W. Zane, *Journeys to the spiritual lands: the natural history of a West Indian religion* (New York: Oxford University Press, 1999) and Bradford Keeney, ed., with photographs by Kern L. Nickerson, *Shakers of St. Vincent* (Philadelphia: Ringing Rocks Press, 2002); for Pocomania, see Martha W. Beckwith, *Black roadways: a study of Jamaican folk life* (Chapel Hill: University of North Carolina Press, 1929).

[4] Born in Grenada in 1897, Tubal Uriah "Buzz" Butler moved to Trinidad in 1922 to work in the oil industry. He played a leading role in the development of a radical working class movement in Trinidad and Tobago which, in turn, infected the entire English-speaking Caribbean in the turbulent 1930s and helped pave the way for the eventual independence of most of the territories.

the time—contested elections as the Eighth Army and they won all eight seats in the population. In looking back, all of this rang true to something that C.L.R. James would write later in *Party Politics*[5] where he made the point (if not in these exact words) that in the English-speaking Caribbean proletarian-oriented forces could, and did, come to power by parliamentary means. Even today, among former colonial peoples like many of us, there's this discussion as to whether or not the "Western" parliamentary system has any validity for our countries; whether we should have multi-parties versus a single party. And anybody really ruminating over the point that James was making would agree with him that that was a fact.

So Joshua and George Charles came to power in this Eighth Army. As young people, a few of us used to go to the central square in Kingstown, the capital of St. Vincent and the Grenadines—a small area with a market place—where, during this campaigning, we would listen to these speakers', especially Joshua and George Charles, anti-colonial and anti-imperialist rhetoric. Many of us were influenced by that. We had heard about Butler before, what was happening in Trinidad going back into 1948—big strikes in the Oilfield Workers Trade Union (1947, 1948)—and some of us, somehow or the other, were tuned to that. In those days we had a Cable and Wireless department and anytime they received the news it would be posted in a case under the gallery of this Cable and Wireless building. So anybody had access to the case and read news about what was happening in Europe and virtually anywhere else. As a matter of fact, going back in time when in 1935 Mussolini invaded Abyssinia (what we know of as Ethiopia today), when the Italian forces were pushed back at some point in time after the invasion took place, a big shout went up as people read news of that event. And it was said that when the administrator or governor who was passing by at the same time heard this shout, he asked the chauffeur to stop and to find out what the shout was about. He found out that Black people were reading those cables and exalting over the fact that Mussolini had suffered a setback in the invasion of Abyssinia. That was the kind of spirit in the country.

George McIntosh, a druggist by profession, used to post a blackboard outside of his doctor shop—that's what they called his place where he sold medicines and that type of thing—where he

---

[5] C.L.R. James, *Party Politics in the West Indies* (San Juan: Vedic Enterprises, 1962).

would write the current news about what was happening either in the country or in the world at large. In addition, what we all noticed is that over that drug store he used to fly a red flag. At that point in time, many of us didn't understand the significance of that red flag but we knew for a fact that that red flag used to be flown on the top of the roof of that drug store. And in 1953, all of this impinged on our faculties. When Joseph Stalin died we remembered that that red flag was flying at half-mast over the drug store. More than that, we also knew that inside of the drug store McIntosh had a big picture of Joseph Stalin in his marshal's uniform. But again, we were just neophytes and we really didn't know the significance of all of that. In 1953 I was just a stripling.

Just to digress, last night we were talking at home about a man called Mr. Rudder whom my father had met going to Trinidad. That man used to send us newspapers from Trinidad all the time and I used to look forward to those papers. In those days my father had a post office box and if at nights, Saturday nights, he took us for a walk he would always go and check his newspaper box and we would all be very delighted. (When I say we, I came out of a home with two other boys. By 1953, it was only two of us at home because my brother had gone to England.) It was all delight to get the *Trinidad Guardian* and I myself would read it. In addition to that, I would go to the library and read papers like the *Daily Gleaner* that used to come in from Jamaica. They used to get that at the library. So you're reading all those things in those ways. Not only that—listening to the BBC [British Broadcasting Corporation.] You had to listen to BBC, seven o'clock at evenings. So I grew up in that atmosphere in a house where that was happening; that was part of one's living there. I would listen to BBC and follow all the news on what was happening in Asia, etc. Not that you could put a certain analysis on it, but all of that remained in your consciousness.

One of the people actually involved in the streets in the 1935 riot[6] was a man that, as boys, we knew by Sheriff and Haile Selassie. He was one of the leaders of the riot and we used to meet him. Much later, a young group in St. Vincent and the Grenadines emerged (they

[6] The 1935 riot in St. Vincent formed part of the series of labour disturbances that swept the entire English-speaking Caribbean between 1935 and 1938. In terms of chronology, they began with a sugar strike in St. Kitts, 1935; continued with a revolt against an increase of Customs duties in St. Vincent, 1935; a coal strike in St. Lucia, 1935; labor disputes in the sugar plantations of British Guiana, 1935; oil strikes in Trinidad and Tobago, 1937; urban riots in Barbados, 1937; and culminated in large-scale strikes and labour rebellions in Jamaica, 1938.

themselves had gone through the Black Power phase and were then moving to what they would call the Scientific Socialist phase).[7] And I remember that my way of trying to orient them a bit in what they were doing was to try to tell them that they must always ground themselves in the local history of the country. I drew up a questionnaire about Sheriff so that they could interview him. But that was a very indirect way of telling them that you have to look around in terms of seeing what has happened under your nose and integrate it with a wider analysis as well. Those guys did a very good job interviewing him and it came out how he got the name Haile Selassie.

But anyway, this fellow Haile Selassie, we would go up and meet him. You would hear that he was one of leaders of the riot. Apparently, Marryshow[8] in Grenada, a contemporary of George McIntosh and an ardent federationist, made a visit to St. Vincent in the 1930s after the invasion of Abyssinia and, in talking about what had happened there, he asked if anybody wanted to volunteer to go and fight on behalf of the Abyssinians. And this man, Samuel Lewis was his name, got up and said he was volunteering and ready to go and from thenceforth he should be known as Haile Selassie. And that's how he got the name.

After the riots took place, Selassie was sentenced to a long prison term and was sent to Grenada to be jailed. People who were labeled ringleaders received prison terms—thirty-forty years. Those terms were eventually reduced and he came back to St. Vincent and, in our time as boys, we just knew him as somebody who was a fish vendor. We didn't know anymore about his history. I just wanted to bring that in to tie in something we were talking about earlier. McIntosh, who had been bracketed with him and tried for that disturbance, was one of the people who formed a trade union in the country, The St.

---

[7] A reference to the Youlou United Liberation Movement (YULIMO), an avowedly Marxist-Leninist grouping that traced its roots to the unrest that ensued in the Caribbean following the arrest and prosecution of the occupants of the computer room during the Sir George Williams Affair in Montreal in the late 1960s. The incident not only galvanized support for the students in Montreal but served as a catalyst for the emergence of social-political groupings throughout the Caribbean. YULIMO was one such mass organization. Members of the YULIMO central committee included Renwick Rose, Ralph Gonsalves, current prime minister of St. Vincent and the Grenadines, Adrian Saunders, Mike Brown, and Casper London.

[8] Theophilus Albert Marryshow was one of the Caribbean's most important early political figures. Using his own newspaper (*The West Indian*) and various forms of political agitation, he advocated for representative government and adult suffrage in Grenada in the early 1900s. He was an elected representative in Grenada for most of his adult life and is also considered one of the founders of the short-lived West Indian Federation where he represented Grenada in the federation parliament's upper house before passing away in 1958.

Vincent Workingmen's Association, in 1936 or thereabout. But McIntosh had already been agitating, virtually since the turn of the century for what you call representative government.

Why representative government? Because, as a consequence of the Morant Bay Rebellion in Jamaica in 1865,[9] the British government decided to completely liquidate whatever semi-representative system that they had instead of extending franchise in Jamaica and any of the other islands. So what you had was naked crown colony rule by just British and local officials. With the exception of Barbados, there were no elections, even on a semi-representative basis, inside of these islands. None at all.

But by the turn of the century agitation began in most of the islands. People were saying that some sort of representative government ought to be returned to these countries. McIntosh was apparently one of many people who were agitating in St. Vincent and representative government associations were formed in most of the islands. By about 1935, the British government was conceding some form of semi-representative government to the islands; you could elect people to the local legislature and those voters were based on who had property and who had a certain income. So McIntosh was one of the people who agitated for all of that and he became a representative in the legislature and carried on agitating both inside and outside the legislature. He formed a trade union, The St. Vincent Workingmen's Association. It is not until I came to Canada and was pursuing a course in Political Science here—"Introduction to Political Science"—that I would come to understand the significance of what they called the Workingmen's Association. Marx had formed an International Workingmen's Association, I think in 1864, and then it dawned on me that we had that in St. Vincent (there was a building they called St. Vincent Workingmen's Association) and then there was some understanding of where all of this thing was coming from.

So a lot of things started to burst open in one's head.

McIntosh was agitating, calling for the deepening of the franchise or responsible government with one person, one vote which was eventually brought into being in 1951. As I said before, it so

---

[9] The Morant Bay Rebellion took place in St. Thomas, Jamaica, in 1865; it was led by Paul Bogle, a Baptist deacon. The rebellion was crushed and its leadership along with hundreds of participants executed. In the aftermath of the rebellion, the Jamaican planters surrendered political power, thus clearing the way for the establishment of Crown Colony rule. For the history of the rebellion, see Gad J. Heuman, *"The killing time": the Morant Bay rebellion in Jamaica* (London: Macmillan, 1994).

happened, paradoxically, that McIntosh lost the elections and this new group of people led by Ebenezer Theodore Joshua and George Charles supplanted McIntosh and carried on this agitation in the country. And it was during the course of that agitation that a lot of us who were now attending the secondary school (I went to the secondary school, the Grammar School, starting in 1950. Pat[10] also went to school there and there was another friend of mine called Kenneth John[11] who is now a regular columnist in a local paper in St. Vincent and the Grenadines (I remember him in particular), we would go to those meetings and listen to those political happenings. So that was the kind of consciousness that was building.

Around the same period we heard that Gairy[12] had emerged in Grenada because Grenada itself now had adult franchise introduced in the country. We heard that Gairy came to power and, as a matter of fact, it was even more turbulent inside of Grenada because there was a sharper struggle going on with the plantocracy in Grenada, culminating in "sky red" as they called it at the time, estates going up in flames. And as a matter of fact, Gairy was actually interned on a warship between Carriacou and Grenada for about three days following those disturbances. Eventually he was released and he went on to win the elections in Grenada. Being partly of Grenadian parentage myself (my mother, having been born in Grenada, came to live in St. Vincent and the Grenadines just after the turn of the century), it turned out that I had an uncle (a brother of my mother) who was a very strong Gairyite and who also played some part in the disturbances. As a matter of fact, when I went to see my uncle in Grenada as a schoolboy in 1952 on an inter-school tournament that

[10] Roberts is referring to his wife, born Patricia Cambridge, who was also from St. Vincent and the Grenadines. An important figure in Montreal's Black and Caribbean community in her own right and an urban planner by profession, she conducted a lengthy study of housing in St. Vincent and the Grenadines. Patricia Roberts passed away in 1998, only two years after her husband. Surviving her are her sons, Rodion and Al, a daughter, Paula-Mae, and two grandchildren, Zachary and Andrew.

[11] Dr. Kenneth John is a lawyer, cricket commentator, author, and lecturer, who writes regularly for the weekly newspaper, *The Vincentian.*

[12] Eric Gairy was a renowned labour leader in Grenada who founded the Grenada Manual and Mental Workers Union in 1950. Premier between March 1967 and February 1974, Gairy became the country's first prime minister when Grenada became independent in 1974. While in office, the quality of Gairy's leadership declined and he became increasingly autocratic. In the 1970s, he used the "Mongoose Gang", a paramilitary security outfit, to carry out state-sponsored violence and intimidation against its opposition. On March 13, 1979, the New Jewel Movement overthrew the Gairy government and established the People's Revolutionary Government (PRG). Gairy took up residence in the United States.

they used to have between the four islands—Dominica, Grenada, St. Vincent, St. Lucia—I remember he took me up to see Gairy.

We used to follow the news on what was going on in the Caribbean. There was Guyana, 1953, when the PPP[13] was under the leadership of Forbes Burnham or, to turn it the other way around, Cheddi Jagan and Forbes Burnham. We were following the news closely when the British government (a Tory government, I think it was Churchill's government) intervened in Guyana and removed the PPP government from power. There were very tenuous links between some people like Joshua in St. Vincent and people in the PPP. Every now and then you would hear that there was a raid in St. Vincent and the Grenadines and you would hear that they were raiding people associated with Joshua for having in their possession a journal called *Thunder*. After a while I realized that *Thunder* was just the organ of the PPP and since the PPP was dubbed a communist outfit there was this hullabaloo in the air.

In the meantime in St. Vincent and the Grenadines, when the Eighth Army came into power, it split in two very early in the game on the basis of whether they were to go to Government House to meet with the administrator on some function. Four said they were not going and four said they were going. The split started on that basis. Eventually Joshua split and he kept on with his agitation in the country and I can say that from that period onward, say from 1952 right up to when I left the country in 1962, Joshua carried on a model of agitprop[14]

in the country. I can count on one hand the Wednesday nights that he missed during that ten-year period. Every Wednesday night that man came to the Market Square, starting maybe with two or three people until eventually he built up a massive following. He was a model in terms of persistence, consistency, and political dedication to that way of life and I think it is a model that many people need to emulate. There are many people who want to come to power instantly

---

[13] The People's Progressive Party (PPP) was founded on January 1, 1950 with Cheddi Jagan as its leader, Linden Forbes Burnham as chairman, and Janet Jagan as secretary. The PPP was elected on April 24, 1953 during the first elections under adult suffrage in the country, winning 18 of 24 seats. The new government immediately began dismantling repressive colonial legislation and repealing anti-labour laws, actions for which it was accused of being communist by the sugar planters and the former ruling elite. On October 9, 1953 the British government suspended Guyana's constitution and used military force to depose the PPP-led government, eventually installing an interim government of its own.

[14] Agitation and propaganda.

and I think that he is one example that one can look to in terms of that steadfastness. Eventually Joshua came to command a majority inside the country. By then he and George Charles had split. They were in a union together called The United Workers, Peasant and Rate-payers Union, which was a variant of the same union that Butler had founded in Trinidad. There was a split and then Joshua formed his own union, The Federated Industrial and Agricultural Workers Union. He was removed from the colonial Executive Council because of his agitation. They said he was a communist and they adduced all kinds of evidence because he had gone to a World Federation of Trade Unions (WFTU) meeting in Vienna.

At that time the WFTU was dubbed a communist union controlled by the Socialist bloc of countries as opposed to the ICFTU, the International Confederation of Free Trade Unions, which had come into being to attempt to supplant the WFTU in which all of the unions inside of the Caribbean had been united following World War Two. That was a casualty of the Cold War—the labour movement in the Caribbean divided on those bases and that type of schism inside of the union movement led to developments in other islands. For example, in Jamaica you had the four Hs—Richard Hart, Ken Hill, Frank Hill, and a man called Arthur Henry—being expelled from the PNP[15] led by Norman Manley after being accused of being communists.

So in 1953 we have these events taking place in St. Vincent and the Grenadines with Joshua coming back and stating in a public square that he had bathed in a marble bath in Vienna and that type of thing.

University of Woodford Square
So we enter about 1954. There's a lot of agitation going on in St. Vincent and the Grenadines with Joshua, in the wilderness of the opposition, being at the centre of it. By 1955, I myself would leave the country to go to school in Trinidad and Tobago. It was in that year that Williams, the deceased Prime Minister of Trinidad and Tobago— Dr. Eric Williams of *Capitalism and Slavery*[16] fame—decided, as he said, "to let down his bucket" inside of Trinidad and Tobago after

---

[15] The People's National Party was founded in Jamaica on September 19, 1938.

[16] Eric Williams, *Capitalism and Slavery* (Chapel Hill: University of North Carolina Press, 1944). In his ground-breaking study, Williams establishes that, notwithstanding resistance to slavery in the Caribbean and

coming out of the losing end of a dispute with the Caribbean Commission where he was employed. He decided to go into politics in Trinidad and Tobago, formed the People's National Movement and by 1956 he was winning elections in Trinidad and Tobago. It's very interesting that a virtually similar occurrence to what happened in Trinidad and Tobago had happened in St. Vincent and the Grenadines in relation to George McIntosh and the emerging new forces led by George Charles and Ebenezer Joshua. From 1946 onwards, Butler virtually had a majority inside of the legislature in Trinidad and Tobago. But that was vitiated or attenuated by other internal politics in the country so he never really had a very strong majority control of the government between 1946 and 1956 when Williams came to power. It happened that when Butler was away in England attending some other function (I think it was having to do with the Crown or the Commonwealth), in his absence, Williams emerged inside the country. So just as when McIntosh was away, new forces emerged in his absence, the same thing happened in Trinidad and Tobago and Williams came to power in 1956.

When Butler returned and heard the news that this Williams and the PNM had come to power, and thinking that he still had tremendous support in the country, he landed on the docks and asked, "Who is this monkey Eric who has assumed power?" And I think the dockworkers turned on him and that gave him a bit of a fit. So he came back into that situation where Williams was now dominant. That was a very harlequin period. That was also another watershed for myself as an individual because I lived through all of that with Williams coming to power, my going to Woodford Square, "University of Woodford Square," as he called it, to listen to Williams speak. You would start to hear phraseology to the effect that a new world is coming into being to redress the balance of the old. And in the higher school level text for English history you would read those same phrases from either Viscount Castlereagh[17] or some high

moral opposition to it in Britain, the British ultimately abolished slavery in the Caribbean for economic and not humanitarian reasons. With the onset of industrialization, slavery was no longer a viable economic enterprise. Williams also leaves little doubt that Britain owed its economic prosperity to the centuries of free labour it exacted from the system of slavery and that modern Britain was built, by and large, on the backs of African slaves.

[17] Viscount Castlereagh, second marquess of Londonderry (1769-1822), as foreign secretary, represented Great Britain at the Congress of Vienna in 1814, where the map of Europe was redrawn after the Napoleonic Wars.

officials in the British government. So Williams brought a whole new approach to political campaigning in Trinidad and Tobago, a very learned, educated approach. He would talk about the 1955 Bandung Conference where China, India, and some of the emergent people in Africa came together and had a meeting in Indonesia out of which would later come the Non-Aligned Movement.

For Williams, in a sense, it was like the Caribbean Commission writ large, that's what Trinidad turned out to be for him. All the knowledge that he had was being brought out into the public arena. He would have a lot of discussions about Aristotle and Plato in relation to some of his opponents, where he would try to get the better of them in the agitprop activity by saying that he could set exams in Aristotle and Plato for them and fail them and that type of rhetoric. So I lived through all of that.

Williams came to power and by then, 1957, there was talk about the Federation. There was a lot of talk since 1948 and even prior to that, and this now culminated in the West Indian Federation. By 1957 I had returned to St. Vincent. As a matter of fact, Williams used to have a press conference every Wednesday night in Trinidad and Tobago and I, back in St. Vincent and the Grenadines and having grown up on Williams and the PNM, continued to follow what was happening.

In 1958 C.L.R. James was invited to the inauguration of the West Indian Federation. They put out a paper—not a big national paper— called the *PNM Weekly*. James was asked to stay and edit the *PNM Weekly*. He was also made the Secretary of the West Indian Federal Labour Party.[18] So he edited this *PNM Weekly* (later it was re-named *The Nation*) that found its way into St. Vincent and the Grenadines. I used to pick up the paper at a store run by a woman called Mrs. Vilna Cox. I used to stay with her brother in Trinidad and Tobago. I would go in that shop to continue my reading and keep abreast of what was happening there. I had a friend, a good friend of mine, a fellow called Mervyn Solomon, who I met in Trinidad. We were in Modern Studies together and we had the same kind of political interests so he would send me a lot of little pamphlets, the PNM speeches of Williams, and

---

[18] The West Indian Federal Labour Party was the governing party in the short-lived West Indian Federation. The 1958 manifesto of the party called for "the creation in the West Indies of a democratic socialist society wherein [are] secured for workers, by hand and by brain, the full fruits of their industry and the most equitable distribution possible[.]" The manifesto also called for strong ties with Puerto Rico, Haiti, Cuba and other countries throughout the Caribbean.

so on, after I returned to St. Vincent and the Grenadines. So I was keeping abreast of all of that.

The West Indian Federation had come into being. James was writing and his work caught my fancy as well. Then there was a tremendous campaign, a model of agitation and propaganda waged by James in *PNM Weekly* over the captaincy of the West Indies team when a fellow like Franz Alexander was made captain ahead of people like Worrell.[19] Also beginning to appear in that paper were some of James' memoirs of George Padmore and things like that. So one's consciousness was being raised by reading and I used to look for the writings of James.

As a matter of fact, there was a bookshop run by a man called George Robinson in St. Vincent and the Grenadines and they used to get a magazine coming out of Jamaica called *New Day*. I remember I used to pick up *New Day* there and it would report when James had gone up to Jamaica to give lectures. They would report the excerpts of these lectures and I used to pick up those kinds of things. I was following James very closely. Another major influence was Nkrumah who had come to power in Ghana. And that was also another watershed. Williams in Trinidad and Tobago and Nkrumah in Ghana would have tremendous effect. A little later on, the Cuban Revolution would take place in 1959. From day one I've been following that revolution, up to today, and I was always very sympathetic to its ideals because they were also about what people like Williams were talking about and what we were studying. In geography they were always talking about the mono-culture, one-crop economy—which was sugar—that the Caribbean was suffering from, that it needed to be transcended and that diversification ought to take place. And now, in the real world, you had people come into power inside of the Caribbean saying that we need all of those things. So in a sense, theory was dovetailing with practice in a certain way. And then it just happened, instinctively, that, being of a particular persuasion, it all went hand-in-hand. I always had that approach to things. It was that type of development that I brought with me when I eventually left the country.

---

[19] Frank Worrell was one of the famous three Ws, Everton D. Weekes and Clyde Walcott being the other two, three of the greatest players in the history of West Indian and world cricket. C.L.R. James launched a campaign in the *Nation* in 1960 when F.C.M. Alexander, a white Jamaican, was named captain over Worrell, despite the fact that Worrell was considered the most able player on the team. Worrell was eventually named captain, largely as a result of James' campaign and popular pressure within the Caribbean.

Cricket Lessons

In relation to my own life, I started traveling very early. In 1947, or thereabout, just after the war, my mother took us to Grenada to see our maternal grandmother who was still alive. She wanted to show her children to her mother so we were taken to Grenada on a boat. I was just about nine and I remember taking a boat called the *Eugenia Allen*, going to Union Island. Union Island is an island of the Grenadines. You see, in those days, say on a Saturday night when you had a lot of the traffickers, these schooners (they were schooners then at the time) would take a lot of the ground provision, pigs, livestock and so on, to be sold in Trinidad. All of this loading up would take place on a Saturday night. All day Saturday these boats loaded down to what you call the plimsoll line (there's a symbol on the boat, a circle, and they call it the plimsoll line) below which you don't load the boat or it's dangerous. And these boats would be loaded down with potatoes, eddoes, ground provision, livestock, pigs, goats, and all that type of thing. Some of them would go through the Grenadines.

Invariably, the captains of these boats would knock around the waterfront drinking all day, and by night they got high. Some of them were nominal captains and they would handle the wheel maybe in the first instance and then turn it over to their mates. It was said that on one voyage there was an old woman called Mrs. Allen (the Allen family was very prominent in Union Island), already in her sixties or seventies, who had to take command of the boat that night because of what was happening on board.

So anyway, we went to Union Island, one of the large islands in the Grenadines. Bequia was the first and then you have a number of other islands until you get to Union Island. Union Island is about the next step going to Carriacou. From Carriacou you go on to Grenada. We had to take a fishing boat—a small boat with a sail—from Union Island, crossing this expanse of water, to go to Carriacou. And I still have the picture of my mother bailing out the water in that boat. The picture never left me.

A fishing boat is just a small boat with a sail. I remember what amazed me at the time was that there were some big pelicans coming out of the air at a tremendous height in the sky, diving down into the water. Seeing something new like that, all of these things strike me. From Carriacou we went by a boat called the *Island Queen* to Grenada and then from Grenada we went up to a place where my mother's family lived in Grenville. Now that place called Paraclete is also very important historically for Grenada because it was in Paraclete where the governor used to live in the 18th century. In March 1795 they had a rising in Grenada under Fedon[20] and the governor at the time, Ninian Home, eventually lost his life. Nobody saw him again at all. Similar developments took place in St. Vincent and the Grenadines led by Chatoyer and Du Vallee,[21] as well as the Maroon rebellion in Jamaica[22]—all this 200 years ago.

In recent times, when there was the untoward event that took place in Grenada with the New Jewel Movement under Bishop and Coard[23]—an internal problem in which Bishop and others lost their lives—and there was all of this horror among many people, some of

[20] Julien Fedon was a "Free Coloured" Grenadian who owned a large coffee and cocoa estate in Grenada. He was chosen by his "Free Coloured" associates to lead a rebellion against the British due to his exceptional leadership skills. Fedon, his associates, and a number of slaves launched an attack against the British in Grenada on March 3, 1795. The rebellion lasted fifteen months and was widespread across the island, causing a number of British casualties. It was eventually crushed by British military reinforcements. Most of the insurgents were killed, though Fedon is said to have escaped and possibly drowned as he attempted to flee to Trinidad by boat.

[21] Chatoyer and Du Vallee were Black Caribs—descendants of African slaves and Carib Indians of St. Vincent and the Grenadines—who launched an attack against the British on the island in March 1795. The attack, which coincided with the Fedon rebellion in Grenada, also involved African slaves and was widespread with the British suffering disastrous defeats. The rebellion ended in June 1796 with the arrival of British military reinforcements. Most of the surviving Black Caribs were transported to Honduras where their descendants remain to this day.

[22] The Maroons were African slaves across the Americas who escaped from colonial plantations to establish their own independent settlements. Masters of guerilla warfare, they employed these tactics to ward off their would-be captors. Roberts is referring to the second of the two Maroon Wars in Jamaica. The first Maroon War began in 1730 and ended in 1739 with the Maroons maintaining their independence when, under the leadership of Captains Cudjoe and Quao, the British sued for peace. The second Maroon War began in July 1795 when two Trelawny Town Maroons were flogged for allegedly killing several tame hogs. The ensuing Maroon outrage, coupled with other grievances, sparked a rebellion against the British, leading to another peace treaty that was signed in December 1795. One of the conditions of the treaty was that those Maroons who surrendered would not be deported from the island. The Maroons were betrayed by the Governor of Jamaica and shipped off to Nova Scotia, Canada and, several years later, transported to West Africa (Sierra Leone) where their descendants still remain. See Richard Hart, *Slaves Who Abolished Slavery, vol. 2, Blacks in Rebellion* (Kingston: Institute of Social and Economic Research, University of the West Indies, Jamaica, 1985).

[23] Maurice Bishop became prime minister of Grenada when the New Jewel Movement seized power on March 13, 1979, overthrowing the corrupt regime of Eric Gairy. The Grenada Revolution captured the imagination of its population and gained popular support around the world as it worked to transform the lives and improve the lot of its population. Bernard Coard, the deputy prime minister of Grenada between 1979 and 1983, was responsible for finance, trade and planning during the Grenada Revolution. In 1983 a major political split developed within the Revolution, primarily between supporters of Maurice Bishop on the one hand, and Bernard Coard on the other. The split resulted in the execution of Maurice Bishop and several

us reminded people that an almost similar event had taken place before in of Grenada.[24]

Grenada seems to have something in its body politic that has pushed it, even politically, in a direction more advanced than some of the other islands. Earlier I talked about the agitation to return responsible representative government to these islands. It is very interesting that the Colonial Office (the chief servant there was a man called Milner) conceded representative government to Grenada ahead of all the other islands in 1919 following the agitation by a representative government association led by Marryshow. Secondly, in terms of the smaller islands moving to political independence, that took place in Grenada in 1974 under the Gairy administration, but again, ahead of some of the other islands that were hemming and hawing. (We know that what people loosely call the "Grenada Revolution" took place in 1979 under the leadership of the New Jewel party government of Bishop and Coard. And they created one of, if not the best governments that the islands have had since slavery.[25] But that was just to digress a bit.)

I went to Grenada again in 1952. By 1953 I was going to St. Lucia as part of a Windward-Leeward combination against British Guyana. I was fifteen at the time, just a boy in short pants, playing cricket for the island of St. Vincent. I played cricket for the island in '53 and

members of the PRG and the implosion of the Grenada Revolution, laying the groundwork for a U.S. invasion of the island in October 1983. Seventeen PRG members were tried and convicted in what has been described as a "kangaroo court", for the murder of Maurice Bishop and several other members of the PRG. With the exception of Phyllis Coard, they continue to serve out their sentences in Grenada.

[24] In his introduction to *Grenada: Island of Conflict* (1984; London and Basingstoke: MacMillan Education Ltd., 1998), George Brizan suggests that the tragic events of October 1983 in Grenada form part of a recurring theme in Grenadian history. According to Brizan, "Grenada's history from 1650 to 1983 has been one of conflicts, either between local groups and classes or between rival imperial cultures. In each case," continues Brizan, "when a major conflict arose, the contradictions between the groups were so antagonistic and the differences so irreconcilable, that it was invariably settled violently." (p. 1)

[25] The Grenada Revolution represented a new stage in Caribbean politics. Grenada was the first country in the anglophone Caribbean to carry out a popular revolution. Upon assuming power, the People's Revolutionary Government established Parish and Zonal Councils to facilitate mass participation in the country's burgeoning political process. The revolution also established a national women's organization in an effort to enfranchise women in the country and took steps towards enshrining its participatory model within the constitutional framework. For the first time in decades, new schools were built, literacy improved, and there was a general sense in the country that, as one Grenadian stated, "the future was coming towards us." Economically, Grenada experienced rapid growth during the revolution, so much so that, according to the then current Attorney General of Grenada, Richard Hart, even the International Monetary Fund viewed the government of Grenada as a model client (Richard Hart, introduction, *In Nobody's Back Yard: Maurice Bishop's Speeches, 1979-1983: A Memorial* (London: Zed Books, 1984), p. xvii).

after that got picked for Windward-Leeward. As a matter of fact, when I went to St. Lucia I stayed in the house of a man, a dentist, by the name of Dr. Carl La Corbiniere because I was the only boy among men. They probably didn't want me to be contaminated with big men in a hotel so they put me in a private home to stay. Later Dr. Carl La Corbiniere would become the federal Minister of Trade and Industry inside of the West Indian Federation.

Nineteen fifty-four, that was my year. I was already in the fifth form, virtually about to sit School Certificate, Cambridge Overseas, and I went to a St. Lucia school tournament early that year, about April. Later in 1954, I played for the Windwards against the MCC, the Marylebone Cricket Club, an English team that was touring the West Indies under the leadership of Len Hutton, the great opening bat for England. I was supposed to go to Dominica that same year to play for the island but my parents wouldn't allow it because they thought that I was losing too much time from school and that I should prepare for School Certificate. But that was no problem to me because I was just a boy and playing cricket was just another passing opportunity so it really didn't mean much to me at the time.

So I was traveling a lot, up and down the area. By then I used to make it my business when I visited these places to simply walk around the town during the day or evening. I would walk around Castries, walk around St. Georges, just to see if people there were any different than the people in St. Vincent and the Grenadines. And that showed me that people everywhere were just about the same—there were no real differences. People's conditions were the same and people were people.

I had experience of larger countries, having gone to New Zealand (1955-56). I saw the impersonal atmosphere that prevailed in these countries and I think I had told myself that I wasn't going to leave St. Vincent again. Even when my friends around me started to leave for England, I said: "You all are going to leave and go. I'm going to stay here because I've been there already. I don't think I relish much what I've seen so I prefer to stay here." I had virtually come to that decision. But then, somewhere along the line, I always had the idea that I wanted to advance my education. Even while playing cricket, the thing that was uppermost in my mind was to get an education, even at School Certificate level. I never wanted to be a rag-doll for anybody and one way to attempt to avoid that was if you had some sort of means by which you can have some control over your life. So if you're educated there's a possibility of getting a job some place. You are not then at the vagaries of other people who want to play games with you.[26] And that was happening in the cricket arena.

I myself in 1948, I think it was, moved from one location, living in the country, to another side of the town and that was very significant because it brought me close to a park[27] where you could go and play cricket and football. It brought me into closer contact with all types of people. And what you discovered there is that even on your teams, your national teams and so on, it was the people from a certain strata who had this tremendous talent. There were elements of that white/black thing that I myself had seen playing cricket because at a certain point in time, to be captain of the island you had to be White. And that happened in St. Vincent right up to 1948; prior to about 1948, you had to be White. Secondly, it began to happen that if you went to the Grammar School there was a tendency to want to make you the captain. And in the Grammar School that I attended from 1950 to 1954, and then going on to QRC [Queen's Royal College] in Trinidad, there was a tendency that if you were the head boy in the school or in sixth form, you should be the captain of cricket, football,

---

[26] As Roberts pointed out in a 1987 unpublished draft essay entitled "A Brief Autobiographical Account of the Cricket Playing of Alphonso Roberts", he was the first from the "smaller islands to play for the West Indies since it was accorded official recognition and test status in 1928..." Hinting as to why he eventually left the game of cricket behind, he continues: "[T]hose who knew Roberts well can vouch for his having been a knowledgeable student of the game...as well as a loyal and unselfish team person, hostile to favouritism, high-handedness and general cussedness in his own quiet way." Roberts goes on to state that he "never meant to make cricket his life's career. He always primarily thought of acquiring at least a half decent education, and then he would see." Finally, he states, "He was also always inclined to have respect for all; to live and let live, not be a rag-doll for anyone, and attempt to maintain an adequate grip on determining the course of his life as far as this was, and is humanly possible." A 1956 programme for the New Zealand tour described Roberts as "an 18-year-old college boy, who has yet to play first-class cricket. He scored 77 for Windward Islands against Australia and as a result of his promise has been awarded a scholarship to Trinidad. He is a fine stroke player." Roberts was among several young players that caught the eye of cricket great Sir Everton Weekes, including Gary Sobers, considered by many to be the greatest player to ever play the game of cricket, and Collie Smith, another great West Indian player who died in a car accident in 1959, long before he reached his prime as a player. Roberts was eventually selected for the West Indies team ahead of Rohan Kanhai, one of the West Indies' great all-time batsmen.

[27] Victoria Park, once the national stadium in St. Vincent and the Grenadines. Roberts's home was virtually on the park grounds, much the same way that C.L.R. James' childhood home faced a cricket pitch, right behind the wicket in Trinidad. Like James, Roberts' close proximity to the cricket grounds permitted him to watch and play organized cricket on a regular basis. The grounds appear to have served as a prism for Roberts, like James, through which he observed and analyzed not only cricket but life and society itself. This was one of the lenses through which he experienced the world at an early age. For an account of the role cricket played in the early life of C.L.R. James see chapter one, "The Window" in James' *Beyond a Boundary* (1963; Durham: Duke University Press, 1993), p. 3.

etc.[28] I was following cricket a lot. I always had an interest in it as a little boy playing in yards. I remember cleaning up a yard when we had birthday parties and getting stumps and putting them down in the yard and playing. I always had an interest in games like soccer too, but I remember, after a while, noticing the way certain players were treated. Once you were not performing you were just simply cast aside. So I never wanted any part of that at all.

So I was able to travel through cricket. I came to the United States in 1958, so I had a familiarity with the States. Playing cricket, I had also gone through some of the Caribbean islands. Although I didn't go to Dominica or Jamaica, I played in Guyana (1956) and went through Antigua and St. Kitts. Visiting New Zealand (1955-56), I went to Suva, the capital of the Fiji Islands. And there I saw the people in Suva with afros like people here in the sixties. As a matter of fact, some of those people played cricket bare feet and in something like a skirt. As well, that trip was very important because certain things in geography became very practical. Going to New Zealand you had to go through the Panama Canal and you saw the operation of the locks and the different levels of the water. You go through from there to the Pacific and when you got out to the Pacific side (it took about three weeks to cross that vast expanse of water) things like water spouts that went from sea to sky, that you read about in physical geography—I saw that right there in the flesh.

[28] Roberts received a scholarship to attend QRC between 1954 and 1957 before returning to St. Vincent. The 1955 QRC Annual Report states: "The college was honoured by the selection . . . of A. Roberts as a member of the West Indian Team to tour New Zealand."

Left: Alfie Roberts and Everton Weekes; *Top*: Gary Sobers, Everton Weekes, Alfie Roberts; *Bottom*: 1956 New Zealand and West Indies Cricket teams

Customs Education

After returning to St. Vincent and the Grenadines from Trinidad and Tobago, I joined the civil service. And this is another thing I'm going to mention that I have never heard anybody talk about. My first assignment in civil service was to work with the Government Secretariat. This was in 1957. The administrator of the country had his office in the Government Secretariat. He lived just a little way outside of the city in the back of the Botanic Gardens at the Government House, a three-storey building that was built some years ago. And what struck me was that when this administrator would come to the Government Secretariat at mornings, everybody would have to stand! I said to myself "Well what's this?" I just couldn't. Instinctively, I just reacted to that. Why should we have to stand when this guy comes in? So I just simply used to get off my haunches, I never stood up straight. And nobody ever spoke about it and I myself never raised it with anybody. But I knew, instinctively, that as long as I was there I was not going to be getting up because I said to myself, "Why is this?"

I spent about three months at the Government Secretariat. This was also very important for me because I got a feel for how the administrative arm of the country operated, because one of my functions at the Government Secretariat was to go and look for the files that were being requested by various departments or ministries. That gave me a clue to the filing system in the country and how the records of the country were kept. I would have to go downstairs in a cellar sometimes if I was looking for a certain file. We see these buildings and never know what is inside of them. There were all of these files going back decades.

So eventually, in my spare time, if there were certain things about the country that I simply thought about, after a while I would sometimes, but very sporadically, go and look and see if I could find the file dealing with some old things. When I went and got the file for a ministry, I would begin reading a lot of the correspondence in the file and got a handle on how some things were being done. At that time George Charles and a fellow called Rudolph Bayne, a merchant, were also in office. But what one would notice in those files is that Bayne would actually write in his own hand his response to whatever subject matter they were dealing with at the time. With respect to George Charles, he would just sign maybe what his Permanent Secretary had prepared because he was not the most literate of people. So I began to see things like that which, to me, was a very good experience.

I began to get a handle on how this administrative thing operated. Then I was transferred to the Customs. I went there as a cashier at first and that was another experience. I always say that you can be born, live, and grow in a country and not know a thing about it. A lot depends on your own experience, especially if you grow up in the city. I was a cashier. Eventually I was transferred to the airport (I was an airport officer) and that exposed me to things that were happening in the country. At that point in time there was a seaplane called the Grumman Goose. It would go as far as Guyana and Trinidad and it came in to a place called Villa, about two or three miles on the windward coast, an area where a certain section of the population, of white skin, lived. Very few people at the time would travel by this plane—largely people of a certain socio-economic bracket.

But that was another experience because, given the whole environment, there was a certain sensitivity given that a lot of people traveling were part of the commercial aristocracy or remnants of the plantocracy. Realizing the environment, I, instinctively, was always trying to develop myself and talk to people in a certain manner and be polite to people. And you found that a lot of those people, if you simply asked them to open their grip, would be annoyed at that. If you are a Customs officer that is part of your duty. You can use your own discretion. You say, "Have you got anything to declare. I would like to see what you have in your suitcase". But the mere fact of you, who they figured to be just an insignificant Black youngster, asking them to open their grip, they got very annoyed at that. We had heard stories that some of those people reported Customs workers and actually got them removed. At one point in time the Financial Secretary in the country was an Englishman and, because of the circles those people moved in, they would call him directly and say "so and so at the Customs has done so and so" and he would call the Collector of Customs and get those guys removed.

The Barnards were owners of one of the largest coconut plantations in the whole world. I'm talking the whole world and I mean that—in small St. Vincent and the Grenadines. I remember a woman, a Barnard, who, when asked to open her grip in the most polite way, became mad as a hatter. She was so mad that when she opened the grip and pulled the belt, she burst it.

In Customs I was asked to take control of one of the two major warehouses in the country for storing goods. That was the senior warehouse. In late 1961 or early 1962 I was asked to take on that assignment because, somewhere along the line, they seemed to have thought that I was bit of a no-nonsense officer. I myself didn't even understand what was happening or what usually goes on in those circles. So anyway, they approached me to go to the warehouse and, in retrospect, I would say that if I knew what was hanging over the warehouse I would have desisted from going.

That experience was all to the good, however, because it tested my own management skills and my ability to interact with different people and work out certain situations. I valued the experience very much because it taught me a lot about how the country was being run economically because, invariably, you have small commercial agents importing ten, twenty, thirty cartons of soap, fifty bags, a hundred bags, two hundred bags of flour. The orthodox rule is that before somebody could even come and inspect their goods they had to go to the bank, get their papers and bring the papers to the Customs where you ensure that their papers are orthodox and inspect the goods to see if there are any shortages. If the agents are satisfied or if there are shortages, they know what quantity of goods they are going to pay for when they prepare their import warrants.

After a while some of the people would come to you and say, "Could you allow me to have five cartons of soap?" even if they don't have their papers from the bank. By then you know people so you know who you will take that chance with. And what eventually dawned upon me was that given the limited money capital with which these people operated, when they came to ask for the five, ten cartons of soap, let's say, they already had a sale for that five cartons of soap which then gives them liquid cash that they could now take to the bank, pay what monies they have to pay, and then eventually pass their warrants. That was an eye-opener for me in terms of how the country was being run. That taught me a lot.

In a job like that you have to take in ships and boats. In those days we didn't have a wharf or pier set up for boats to come up alongside a pier and deliver goods. The boat stayed a bit out in the harbour and you had lighters that brought the goods ashore. In those days, probably still continuing, you had English boats or Dutch boats that brought in cargo from Holland and all over the place. They unload for three days and three nights and in those days you had one Customs officer in the warehouses. During the day you come to work.

You began work at 8:30 am and your day finished by 4:30 pm. In between that period you delivered goods from the warehouse because people would come everyday to take out goods. But you had to take the cargo in as well from the unloading boats. So you're tallying in stuff and you're delivering at the same time and there is just one man in the warehouse. This goes on for three or four days and nights, 4:30 pm until 7:00 pm, and I or the warehouse officer would have to stay. You take supper, come back and reopen the warehouse by 8:00 pm and work until the next morning, say about until 7:30 am. You close the warehouse, go home, and you have to come back to open the warehouse by 8:30 am. That goes on for three days and three nights, four days and four nights, or one day and one night, but you get paid overtime. You chalk it up. You're asked to do an assignment and you carry it out.

I was still very naïve in that when I was asked to go to the warehouse I was then what you call a class-two clerk. When you entered the service you entered as a class three clerk, then you go to class two, and then you become a class one clerk. I was already at class two level and when they came to me to go to the warehouse they said to me, "Well look. In time you'll get promoted," because to be in charge of the warehouse, that is a class one clerk's job. "In time you'll be given the class one clerk pay but overtime will compensate in the meantime."

I found out there was a scandal hanging over the warehouse where apparently some skullduggery might have been going on with whoever was in charge of the warehouse before I got there. After a while I realized that but I was already there. The man in charge of the Customs at the time knew what was up and, in a sense, I saw what was happening. This is one of the hazards of being in charge of anything. By virtue of being head of the department, somewhere along the line, even if you don't have any knowledge of what is happening at the subordinate level, the buck stops with you. So whatever was happening in the department would reflect on the man who was in charge, and therefore he, too, was working to clear up whatever mess existed, since it would reflect on his department.

So I found myself in a bit of hot water because there was a mess, a racket, some sort of misappropriation of goods. When you tally in your goods you have to check the goods with the manifest. The ship has a manifest of the goods that it's bringing for that country and you have to see if those coincide and then you write up in a register what you receive. But like in every sphere of life, you can do a lot of things. You could work out deals with people but the only thing is that once you make your entries you ought to have a warrant to indicate that if you've gotten one bail of cloth, that this bail of cloth has been paid for and then you have to mark that bail of cloth against that warrant. What could also happen is that, as a warehouse officer, you may not be at fault because you have people doing all kinds of things. You have pilfering and if you're not sharp, people will carry out a bail of cloth on you. I had to learn that after a while. You have to learn the tricks because, for example, with a shipment of flour there's a way of packing two-to-one and on the trailer you take out about twenty-five sacks of flour.

Now if you check the flour by the side—one, two, three, four, five, and five by five is twenty five—instead of counting laterally, you better look from the front or the back of the thing as well because there might be two extra bags in the middle so when you think it's twenty-five, actually twenty-seven bags have gone on you. And then eventually somebody might come and ask, "But where is... I had fifty bags of flour here," because the people who come to clear the flour, they themselves work out the deal with somebody they're going to sell the two bags of flour to. So you end up with forty-eight instead of fifty bags of flour and then eventually they'll put the onus on you. There are tricks in the trade as with everything. You might not necessarily be involved in any skullduggery but you could also be too. And you have to figure out the best way to get out of it. And these warrants are checked as well. You have an audit that comes later on where people are checking the one versus what is entered in the book and if there's some discrepancy, they come to you.

I learnt a lot of things going to the warehouse. It was there where you saw the proletarians who were working at that lower level, bringing cargo into the warehouse, things like that. You saw that their mores and folkways were different to people of a certain other strata. For example, these men would joke among themselves and say, "You're down here working. Some man is up in your house with your wife." They would make fun among themselves about that. Now, at another socio-economic stratum people don't say those things (though they might say them behind your back). I began to learn that different strata of people deal with things in different kinds of ways and that was a tremendous eye-opener for me. All of that went into my own development and my sensitivity to what was happening in the country and, plus, I just instinctively had a certain way about how I felt certain things should happen in the country.

My warehouse became like a marketplace for ideas. There was a man called Sutherland and he loved to discuss certain things so we all used to discuss a lot. About two o'clock people would leave certain parts of town and come to that warehouse because there was discussion going on about all kinds of things. Having been an earlier follower of the Cuban Revolution, I remember reading somewhere that a book on the Cuban Revolution had been written by a man called Hubert Matthews who worked with the *New York Times*. He said that he had gone into the mountains of the Sierra Maestra. When Castro and the others were fighting, he interviewed them and wrote this book. I wrote away to the *New York Times* and the man sent me a copy of the book, *The Cuban Story*,[29] I think it was. And I remember there was a particular man who came to the warehouse to clear his goods, a man who used to bring his warrant. He was a man who asked no quarter and gave none. He had that kind of approach about him. He saw me with this book and his eyes lit up to it and he expressed an interest. There were some other people who came to the warehouse. I remember another person expressing a certain interest in people like Cheddi Jagan's PPP (Guyana). And what all of that began to tell you is that you don't know what people are thinking and you can't judge them by the way they look and how they carry themselves. Things like that impacted me.

We used to have free-wheeling discussions in the warehouse and then one day this fellow Sutherland asked the question, "How is it that Black people have never made anything like cars?"

Nobody could answer. Nobody could answer and, quietly, I vowed to myself that I would have to get to the bottom of that. I must have been thinking about leaving the country by then because I had a friend who once worked at the Customs. He came to Montreal by 1961 and he sent me a copy of the bulletin or the prospectus from Sir George Williams University and then I think I made the decision to come. I then vowed to myself that I would have to get to the bottom of the question of why Black people never made cars. That was one of the things uppermost in my mind when I left the country, that I would have to get to the bottom of this thing with Black people.

---

[29] Hubert Matthews, *The Cuban Story: A Personal Interpretation of the Cuban Revolution and its Impact on the United States and on Latin America* (New York: George Braziller, 1961).

In 1963 I spent the summer in the United States. I stayed with a friend of mine. My father was his godfather and he kindly consented that I could stay there with him. So I spent the summer with him in New York. But I was familiar with New York because I'd gone there in 1958 for a tournament with a cricket team. I stayed higher up in Harlem with a Jamaican woman named Mrs. Tully, Irma Tully, and her daughter (Elaine, I think her name was). Leaving an island like St. Vincent and the Grenadines where there are certain very marked demarcations—where you don't find churches, taverns, and clubs combined—in New York, I was very consternated because you would go to New York and see that. That had an impact upon me. Not only that. What I saw is that the place doesn't sleep at all. It's just one continuous activity.

Somehow—I can't remember how—I discovered before I left home that there was this place called University Place Bookshop in New York, and I went there and started to hunt for information. I picked

Customs Officer Alfie Roberts on right

up books like *The Black Jacobins*[30] and then *The World and Africa*[31] by Du Bois and in reading that book I said, "Ah, there it is!" and I was at peace with myself. That was a source of strength. Somehow or the other that gives you a source of strength.

Higher Learning

My father was very up on reading. He always said you should read. He was the man who would tell you to go and join the library. "Go and pick up a book and read." So that kind of thing was there. My mother too, quietly, would agitate, and when I say agitate I mean she made sure you go to your school, but never interfered with us. Nobody had to sit us down and say, "Do your work" or do this and do that. I worked at an average level but I think it is just a certain instinctive thing with me. For example, I had a brother who, if you had a foreign team come to St. Vincent to play soccer, he would want to root for the foreign team and I just couldn't stand that. Instinctively, I couldn't stand that at all. Somehow, things like Carnival, all of that type of activity . . . it's difficult to explain it but it had an impact upon me. When the steel band came into being I followed its development. I used to be in yards where it was happening. I witnessed how they marked the pans out and things like that. All of that kind of thing had a certain something for me. It is very difficult to articulate that now. So it is that type of development—what happened in 1951, what happened before, reading, and the West Indian Federation—that I brought to Montreal.

As I said, I had decided that I wasn't going to leave St. Vincent and the Grenadines but I had always had that desire to improve, to obtain higher education. So when my friend, Ashford Lewis, sent me a copy of that Bulletin and I looked at it, I was in two minds. I noticed that you had to pursue literature (English literature) as part of the course of study and I was never overly fond of literature. I said, "Oh my God!" Then I said to myself, "Why should I leave here?" By then we had moved from one part in the city to another area and the new site was a nice one. The whole harbour was in front of me. I was working. I was starting to work for $60 a month at the time. I gave

[30] C.L.R. James, *The Black Jacobins: Toussaint L'Ouverture and the San Domingo Revolution* (1938; New York: Vintage Books, 1989).

[31] W.E.B. Du Bois, *The World and Africa: An Inquiry into the Role that Africa has Played in World History*, (1947; New York: International Publishers, 1965).

$20 contributive to my home and if I had to buy a pants length in those days it cost twenty bucks. And there was George Robinson, the bookshop man. They used to get the papers from Trinidad so I used to buy them every week. You had to find money for that; then you save some money. By the end of the month you had no money. As a matter of fact, I never saved in any bank at all. I never put my money in a foreign bank. I used to save in the Treasury. There were saving possibilities in the Treasury and I used to save my money in the treasury, just instinctively patriotic that way. I'd never go to a bank. And as a matter of fact, you got a better interest rate in the Treasury as well.

I said to myself, "I can't take on that. I'm living here comfortably. I think maybe I'll buy a car, live cool, go to my job, and just relax here." I said that's what I would do. But then I said to myself, I could buy the car today and by tomorrow I hit it and I would be back to square one. And so I just weighed it up. I said if I went and got an education, it would be there for whatever that meant.

Moreover, there was the possibility of getting no pay leave from the civil service. I thought I would come, get a degree, and rejoin the civil service in order to have an unbroken record. When that was put to the Chief Secretary at the time, he indicated, in a very elliptical way, that if you apply for this type of concession and don't get it, you resign. So I decided to do that. I will leave. If I don't get the no paid leave, I'll still go and study. That's how I left the country.

But I had no teleological reason for getting that education. I mean, it was just one of the things I thought I should get, but it wasn't a stepping stone for me to get a better job anywhere. I never thought in those terms. Anyhow, I said: "I'm going to move," and so I did. And I must say that I have not regretted having done that at all.

The "Quiet Revolution"

By 1962 when I came to this country, there was gestation in the society. Armories were being besieged and every other day you would hear that a bomb had been put in a post box. What we understood then was that the FLQ was responsible for those incidents.[32] As well,

---

[32] The Front de libération du Québec (FLQ) was a socialist-oriented nationalist group fighting for Quebec independence. The FLQ was influenced by nationalist movements of the sixties. In his *The White Niggers of America*, Pierre Vallières, one of the leading spokespersons for the FLQ, draws heavily on the Black Power movement in the United States as well as the works of Amilcar Cabral and Frantz Fanon, particularly Fanon's *Wretched of the Earth*, for inspiration. Beginning in 1963, the FLQ carried out a series of bomb attacks and

we understood in retrospect that something called the Quiet Revolution[33] was then underway in Quebec. There was a change of government. A Liberal government came into being, I think in 1960, under a man called Jean Lesage, supplanting the Union Nationale government led by a man called Duplessis who ran a pretty conservative, anti-communist administration. As a matter of fact, even at this point in time, at the end of 1959, there was no separate ministry of education [from the church] in Quebec and this Liberal government decided that it wanted to update Quebec society, to modernize it and bring it more into the temper of the modern world.

But, as I said, by 1962 I met bombs being thrown. I also discovered a book called *Why I am a Separatist* by a fellow called Marcel Chaput[34] and in reading that book, I discovered that the point was made that if Guinea could become independent then why not Quebec? Now Guinea, as we know, resumed its political independence in 1959 as the result of a referendum that was held in Guinea.

That was the method that was advocated by the French metropolitan government, that one way by which a country under the colonial control of France could become independent was by way of a referendum. You have a referendum where the people are asked to vote: "Do you want to be independent, yes or no?" And Guinea was the only country in that francophone relationship, or Francophonie relationship, that voted: "No, we don't want to continue the relationship with France."

More than that, the Cuban Revolution would take place in 1959 as well. The Algerian Revolution, which had started in 1954, was in its last year or two and by 1961, independence was conceded to the Algerians. The writings of Fanon from Martinique (who had joined the

acts of violence against what they considered to be symbols of their oppression. In 1970 the Liberal Canadian government of Pierre Trudeau invoked a state of emergency, the War Measures Act, following the kidnapping of James Cross, a British diplomatic trade representative and Pierre Laporte, the Quebec Minister of Labour, by members of the FLQ. Laporte was eventually found dead and several members of the FLQ were arrested, tried and convicted for his murder.

[33] The Quiet Revolution began with the accession to power of the Quebec Liberal Party under the leadership of Jean Lesage in June 1960, ending a twenty-four year reign, known as the "Dark Ages", of the ultra-conservative Union Nationale led by premier Maurice Duplessis. Lesage instituted reforms in education and other public and private institutions, which broke both the British and the Catholic Church's stranglehold on Quebec society and brought the French Quebecois into economic and political prominence.

[34] Marcel Chaput, Tr. Robert Taylor, *Why I am a Separatist* (Toronto: Ryerson Press, 1962).

Algerian Revolution)—*The Wretched of the Earth,*[35] etc.— were making the rounds. And with this new climate in Quebec, there was a lot of agitation on the campuses, especially at the University of Montreal, then the major French-speaking institution of higher learning here. People were infected by the Civil Rights Movement in the United States. As we know, in 1955, Rosa Parks had said she was not getting up.[36] That activity in the United States had an effect in Canada, especially here in Quebec. One result of that was a book by Pierre Vallières called *The White Niggers of America.*[37]

So all of this was happening and there was a certain conjuncture of events. We are talking about the agitation, the effervescence, the emerging to the fore of the problems that Black people were having and were publicly agitating to have redressed in the United States; we are talking especially about the Cuban Revolution in 1959 with its bearded, olive green-clad combatants filling the newspaper pages and the works of guerilla warfare by Che Guevara making the rounds; we're going back to Nkrumah in 1957—the independence of Ghana; we're talking about Guinea in 1959; the works of Fanon. All of this had a tremendous impact on what was happening here in Quebec and I walked into all of it.

The question of violence that people try to use in a very alarmist way was up in the air and a lot of students were very enamoured with that type of option. And that is why people in the FLQ were opting for that method of activity. There's no doubt at all that what was happening in Africa and what was happening in terms of Black people in the United States, those developments had a very significant impact here, especially in Quebec, and you rarely find any allusion to this.

I remember a fellow called Richard Fid from Jamaica, one of the few people that you could meet on the campus that, in between lectures, you could stand and talk with about what was happening— what was happening in the Caribbean and what was happening generally. Gradually some other people started to come in, people

---

[35] Frantz Fanon, *The Wretched of the Earth* (1961; New York: Grove Press, 1968).

[36] A reference to Rosa Parks' famous act of civil disobedience in refusing to cede her seat to a white passenger in Montgomery, Alabama. Parks was promptly arrested by the local authorities and the ensuing outrage helped to provide the spark that ignited the modern Civil Rights movement.

[37] Pierre Vallières, *The White Niggers of America* (Toronto: McClelland and Stewart Limited, 1971).

with whom I would then be able to relate in terms of what was happening. We had another friend here called Kerwyn Morris from St. Vincent and the Grenadines. He came in 1961, the year before I arrived and we began to do a lot of work on Africa.

I'll never forget that before leaving the country I had stopped going to the cinema in St. Vincent and the Grenadines entirely because there was something irking me. Every now and then you had these pictures, occasional pictures of Black people in a loincloth running around in these films and, instinctively, I couldn't hack it. And I remember I stopped going to cinema because I said to myself that it couldn't be that Black people just emerged from a hole in the ground. That is what it sounded like, that Black people somehow just emerged from some hole in the ground with this loincloth. It never made any sense to me.

Kindred Souls

I came here in 1962 to go to school full-time, to do an undergraduate degree at Concordia.[38] I began to meet one or two people on the campus but nothing really coalesced and came together until 1965. By 1965 some other people started to drift in here. There was a young man called Franklyn Harvey. He had come in to go to school at McGill. He was already an engineer. He had come here to do a Masters in planning. There was another young man by the name of Hugh O'Neale who was a rising young economist. He had just graduated from UWI [University of the West Indies] and he had helped prepare a document on the situation in the Eastern Caribbean[39] with a woman called Carleen O'Loughlin who was with the University of the West Indies. He went through the islands and garnered all the statistics and figures to put that report together. He was a Grenadian who came here to do a doctorate and it turned out he was cousin to my wife Patricia Cambridge. So these other people started to come and I began to meet other people around the place.

The impetus for what was to make up the Conference Committee on West Indian Affairs came from these other people who were

[38] Present-day Concordia University was known as Sir George Williams University up until 1974 when it merged with Loyola College and assumed its new name.

[39] Carleen O'Loughlin, with statistical appendices by H. O'Neale, *A Survey of Economic Potential and Capital Needs of the Leeward Islands, Windward Islands, and Barbados* (London: Her Majesty's Stationary Office, 1963).

Top: Alfie and Pat Roberts, Montreal 1960s; Bottom: Alfie , Montreal, 1963

themselves coming in. In 1965 we had a visit in the person of Robert (Bobby) Hill, a Jamaican and a friend of his, another Jamaican fellow.[40] I can't remember his name off the bat but he used to do some part-time teaching at, I think, the University of Montreal. But he seemed to go backward and forward between Ottawa and Montreal and they came down from Ottawa. There was a fellow by the name of Ewart Walters, too (he's now back in Ottawa, following the demise of the Manley government). He worked in the sphere of communications, journalism. At the time, he was in Ottawa.

Also studying in Ottawa around that period was Anthony Hill, a cousin of Bobby Hill. Anthony was the son of Ken Hill, one of the Four Hs expelled from the PNP. This son of his was also doing a Masters in public administration at Carleton University. Carleton was a university that, under the Columbo Plan—one of these UN-type plans where, under the auspices of the UN, courses were offered to civil servants in the colonial empire, or former colonial empire—you could come and upgrade your skills. A lot of civil servants from Asia, the Caribbean, and Africa would come on these one-year scholarships in public administration and Carleton was apparently fairly famous for this course in public administration. I myself would eventually go to Carleton and pursue some graduate work later on. That would be 1965-66 after graduating from Sir George Williams University (now Concordia University).

But anyway, it was in 1965 that Bobby, or Robert Hill and his cousin Anthony visited Montreal and I think they met with Ivan Morrison who was in charge of a Jamaican Association here. Bobby and the others apparently had either heard of him or knew him, and they came to see him because they had this idea (I don't know where that idea came from) about organizing a conference. By coming here, Bobby got in touch with those us who were already here. Rosie Douglas from Dominica was here. He had come in 1961. He had come to Guelph to pursue a diploma in agriculture, because Guelph was famous for that, and then he transferred here to Montreal and was studying at Sir George Williams.

Bobby and Anthony Hill came out of a bit of a political tradition and that kind of tradition was motivating them in this direction as

---

[40] The "Jamaican fellow" was Barry Myers, brother of Ivanhoe Morrison who was an original member of the Conference Committee and in whose house the Committee initially met. Myers met Robert and Anthony Hill in Ottawa where he taught at Ottawa University's Economics Department.

well. They were coming out of Jamaica where there was activity at a certain level going on. So this group of people and some other kindred individuals were here and I served my apprenticeship in the Conference Committee on West Indian Affairs because there were people like Bobby and Rosie here. Rosie was a busybody, one could say. He knew a lot more people in the society and how to get things done. So we were like a supporting cast but we had our own independent ideas as well.

There was a group of people at that time going to school here at McGill. Some of them were pursuing Master and Ph.D. studies at the university and they were also part of the New World circle. *New World Quarterly* was a journal that came out of the University of the West Indies with people like Lloyd Best,[41] James Millette,[42] Norman Girvan,[43] and people of that ilk. They were bringing out a journal called *New World Quarterly* and they were grappling with Caribbean issues. So when I came here those people, already at McGill, had their own circle. But then this other circle of ours emerged.

When I came here I was already going past and transcending Williams and Manley because by then, somehow, I began to see their limitations. They used to have debates in the parliament in Trinidad and the Opposition, led by the Democratic Labour Party which was very much Indian predominant, had a man called Seukeran who used to speak a lot in the Chamber. After a while, Williams took to taking out his earphone in the parliament.[44] That turned me off Williams. Something about that just turned me off because I think that I was always like an underdog person in the sense that I couldn't

---

[41] Trinidadian economist Lloyd Best was associated with McGill University's Centre for Developing-Area Studies in the 1960s; he was the leading force behind Tapia House in Trinidad, an intellectual-based organization which, among other things, served as a constant critic of the policies of Eric Williams' government and attempted to put forward an alternative vision of development for the Caribbean.

[42] Trinidadian historian James Millette served as the chair of the New World Group from 1964 to 1968. He was the founder of *Moko*, a popular opposition newspaper, and taught for more than twenty years at the University of the West Indies, St. Augustine campus, in Trinidad. Millette was one of the first intellectuals to publicly criticize Prime Minister Eric Williams in the sixties. He served as the Extra-Mural Tutor at the University of West Indies in St. Vincent and Dominica from 1960 to 1961 where he met Alfie Roberts and encouraged him to continue his studies.

[43] In the 1967 Conference Committee program, the economist Norman Girvan was also listed as a member of the Conference Committee. From 1966 to 1973 he served as a lecturer at the University of West Indies, Mona Campus, Jamaica. He is currently the Secretary General of the Association of Caribbean States.

[44] Dr. Williams used a hearing aid due to a hearing impediment.

deal with any kind of contemptuous, high-handed activity at all. I had a sense of fair play and justice, irrespective of who you were. I believed that people should deal with each other in a certain way. So all of those things were already instinctively in me, very quietly so. (People didn't know what you were thinking. We all can't know what people are thinking unless we get close to them.)

When Williams came to power, he also took over the policies that were being carried out in Puerto Rico—the Puerto Rican Operation Bootstrap problem. Eventually I think the New World people began to coin the phrase "industrialization by invitation," where you set up these factory shells and you invite foreign investors in, give them concession, and tax-free holidays. Williams was advised by Professor Arthur Lewis, one of the economic gurus of the Caribbean, and another man called Teodoro Moscoso in Puerto Rico. Manley had been doing the same thing in Jamaica since 1955 when the PNP had come to power after being in the political wilderness for about ten or more years.

What also helped me to begin to question Williams even before I left the Caribbean was that in 1960, when they were still attempting to work out the West Indian Federation, Williams and Manley met in Antigua and Barbuda to clarify some economic aspect in the relationship. It had something to do with oil refining. And following the meeting, in a public meeting in Antigua and Barbuda in 1960, Williams made the allusion to Cuba to the effect that he didn't see the point in changing one Beelzebub for another. Once I read that speech and picked up that it was an allusion to Cuba, I had an inkling of what road he was on and that is one of the first signs that began to turn me away from Williams because I think it was, to me, an anti-communist inference and I think time has borne that out. I already had a certain instinctive notion of a certain kind of development, about what should be happening. Williams introduced a Five Year Plan, and then a second Five Year Plan. Somewhere along the line, it dawned upon me that nothing profound was happening. First Five Year Plan—nothing. Second Five Year Plan. Just instinctively, something told me that nothing was happening.

The other thing I must say is that Nkrumah came to power, as I said, in Ghana in 1957, and we were following Nkrumah. When he turned the country into a one-party state, many of us were, in a sense, sympathetic to that. But after a while that began to trouble me because Nkrumah had begun to say things like "the CPP is Ghana and Ghana is the CPP"[45] and something didn't ring true and right about that. How could the CPP, which was a political organization of one group of people, arrogate Ghana unto itself? It just didn't make any sense to me, something wasn't quite right about that. And how could the single-party represent the entire views of any country? That didn't make any sense to me either because there's another group of people who could have different ideas than this one single-party. That troubled me and I quietly ditched the whole idea of the single-party. I said to myself, if it came into being as a result of voting people into power, fine and dandy. But what Nkrumah eventually did, I think, was consciously to turn the state into a one-party state. I got the impression that he thought he was being left behind by some other countries in Africa that began to adopt the one-party system and he then moved in that direction, no matter the problems he had in the country.

So the single-party was not something that I would ever stand up and advocate. Not at all, and, as I said earlier on, up to today, it doesn't make any sense to me that even people who say they're progressive, on the left, say that the Western parliamentary system is not for us. I've never agreed with that. Because to me, the Western parliamentary system that people say is not for us—W-E-S-T-E-R-N P-A-R-L-I-A-M-E-N-T-A-R-Y, to spell it—those are only letters and words. The people, individuals themselves, and how they create and conduct themselves is what matters; that is what tells you something about a system. To me, something called a system is only a word on paper. It is the people who are supposed to represent that system who give it content and that content could either be bad, good, or indifferent. So that was always my approach. In addition to what I am saying, C.L.R. James had made the point that Bustamante[46] in Jamaica had come to power with masses of people supporting him through the parliamentary system where people voted. It happened in Trinidad and Tobago and right throughout the Caribbean:

[45] The Convention People's Party (CPP) was founded by Kwame Nkrumah in 1949 when he broke away from the more conservative United Gold Coast Convention led by the intellectual J.B. Danquah. Through the CPP, Nkrumah led the country to self-government in 1951 and political independence in 1957.

[46] Alexander Bustamante, the Jamaican labour leader, founded the Jamaican Labour Party (JLP) in 1943 after parting ways with his cousin Norman Manley and the People's National Party. Both Manley and Bustamante petitioned the British government for independence and, following an election in which the JLP was swept into office, Bustamante became the first prime minister of an independent Jamaica on August 6, 1962.

Bradshaw[47] in of St. Kitts coming to power in the late thirties, early forties; Bird in Antigua;[48] everywhere in the Caribbean. In other parts of the world, what a lot of people were hoping for is that the ordinary people, workers and peasants, would give them support. Here was that version applied to the Caribbean with all of these people coming to power. But what became more than clear afterwards was that they didn't know what to do. Well, not that they didn't know, but that the conception that they had in terms of what to do with that power was, in a sense, one could say, misplaced.

Instinctively—nobody put that in me in any way—looking for information in terms of how to understand the world in which I was living and to clarify things, I moved to reading a lot of socialist literature—especially by Marx, eventually Engels, and Lenin. And up to today, I find that what they were saying makes a lot of sense.

The Conference on West Indian Affairs

So Bobby and Anthony Hill had come from Ottawa with their background out of Jamaica. Anthony Hill was the son of Ken Hill. He was a very bureaucratic character with a flair for organization. He was a very good footballer. They tell me he's one of the best soccer players that Jamaica produced and he had gone to England earlier with a West Indian soccer team. But on meeting and getting closer to him—because he was still in his second year when I eventually went to Carleton—and observing him, I realized he had a very bureaucratic flair and a very cynical approach in terms of what he thought could be done with many things. But he was a good organizer. We all hooked up and we formed this Conference Committee on West Indian Affairs and organized a conference at the University of Montreal called "The Shaping of the Future of the West Indies".

Apparently, when greetings were being brought to the 1965 conference—the conference on "The Shaping of the Future of the West Indies" with George Lamming as guest speaker[49]—there was an

---

[47] Robert Bradshaw was a labour leader in St. Kitts-Nevis who came of age in the social turbulence that gripped the Caribbean in the 1930s. In 1967 he became the first premier of the Associated States of St. Kitts, Nevis, and Anguilla.

[48] Vere Bird was a labour leader in Antigua and founder of the Antigua Labour Party in 1950. Bird became the first prime minister of Antigua and Barbuda when it gained independence on November 1, 1981.

[49] In the opening remarks of his speech at the conference, George Lamming, the Barbadian novelist, poet, and lecturer stated: "I don't know whether you realize what a very significant honour it is for me to be here

individual who got up in the conference and said he brought greetings as the lone wolf from Nova Scotia. He turned out to be Tim Hector.[50] I had never met or heard of Tim before but it turned out that Bobby had met him the previous year in Toronto where Tim was spending his summer vacation and Bobby invited him to the conference. So there is this coming together with people like Bobby Hill, Rosie, Ann Cools, Hugh O'Neale, and Alvin Johnson. After that conference Alvin Johnson and Hugh O'Neale, going to Toronto to relate and discuss this conference, or coming conferences, lost their lives on the highway, a tragic loss. Then the whole idea of bringing James now came to the fore. Bobby and I had known about James and I think Bobby somehow had information on James through his relations in Detroit and he started to get us some information on the group that James had belonged to.[51] So we started to read a lot about that stuff. In 1966 we had a conference called "The Making of the Caribbean People", with James as guest speaker.[52] And we brought in people like

in these circumstances because although I have done a great deal of traveling in the last 15 years both in Africa and North America, this is actually the first time in my career as a writer that I have ever been the guest of a West Indian organisation." Lamming went on to state: "I would like also to let you know that what you are doing here tonight has many echoes in London and for many of your compatriots who work in various activities throughout Africa. You are in fact in a sense operating on a world scale." Lastly, Lamming stated, "I want also, I think, to congratulate you on what I believe is the first conference of this kind. I sincerely hope that you could achieve another first by seeing to it that the next is held on Caribbean soil" (George Lamming, "The Shaping of the Future of the West Indies", *New World*, Vol. II, No. 2, 1966). This edition of *New World* also includes a resume of the October 1965 conference itself. Lamming's speech was also published by the Conference Committee in their October 1967 Caribbean Conference bulletin. Robert Hill of the Conference Committee also organized a lecture tour for Lamming which included the following engagements in Canada and the United States: New York University; The American Society of African Culture, New York; Fisk University, Nashville Tennessee; University of Indiana, Bloomington; University of Toronto; and McGill's Centre for Developing-Area Studies, Montreal. According to Robert Hill, the Conference Committee's work with Lamming served to reconnect him to the Caribbean and helped to resuscitate his career.

[50] A native of Antigua and Barbuda, Leonard Tim Hector was a philosophy student at Acadia University in Wolfville, Nova Scotia at the time.

[51] The Facing Reality group was the successor to the Johnson-Forest Tendency. "Johnson" and "Forest" were pseudonyms for C.L.R. James and Raya Dunayevskaya, respectively, the two founding members of the Tendency. Other members of the group included Grace Lee Boggs and Martin Glaberman. This small Marxist organization produced a number of original works of Marxist theory and analysis. In addition to the *Invading Socialist Society* (1947; Detroit: Bewick Editions, 1972), other publications of the group during this period include *Notes on Dialectics* (James, 1948), *Mariners, Renegades and Castaways* (James, 1953), *Every Cook Can Govern* (James, 1956), and *Facing Reality* (James, Grace Lee, and Pierre Chalieu, 1958). The Conference Committee established ties with the Facing Reality group in the mid sixties.

[52] See C.L.R. James, *The Making of the Future of the West Indies* (London: Bogle and L'Ouverture Publications, 1968). *New World*, Vol. III, No. 4, 1966 also includes a version of the paper presented by Lloyd

Members of the Conference Committee on West Indian Affairs
From L-R: Franklyn Harvey, Robert Hill, Alfie Roberts, Tim Hector

Norman Girvan, economics lecturer at UWI, James Millette, and people of that ilk. Tim, who was going to school in Wolfville, Nova Scotia (I think he was doing an honours program in philosophy) obviously became a part of us and started to come and spend his summer vacations here in Montreal. Franklyn Harvey was already here because he had been a friend of Hugh O'Neale and Hugh O'Neale being my cousin in-law, we got to know Franklyn. Franklyn came with a certain consciousness too because he studied at UWI and as a matter of fact, he had a paper that he had written on the West Indian Federation, a paper that I still have up to today. So he was of that thinking nature about the social-political situation in the Caribbean. I think that we were just like kindred souls who came together and we took off from there, organizing these conferences. But as I said, by then, I myself had gone past people like Williams and Manley, but I remember that when we started to discuss among ourselves, some of the guys were still stuck at the PNP and PNM stage with Williams.

Best, "Independent Thought and Caribbean Freedom", at the 1967 conference. In an unpublished interview conducted on July 18, 1995, Gloria Simmons, a member of the Conference Committee on West Indian Affairs, suggests that the Committee came under investigation by Canadian authorities as a result of their relationship with C.L.R. James.

CONFERENCE ON WEST INDIAN AFFAIRS 1966

The Making of the Caribbean Peoples

McGILL UNIVERSITY — LEACOCK AUDITORIUM

OCTOBER 7-9

25 cents

PROGRAMME

The Making of the Caribbean Peoples

Friday — October 7

6.00 - 8.00 p.m.	Registration — Leacock Auditorium
8.00 - 10.00 p.m.	Chairman's Address Guest speaker, C.L.R. James
10.00 - 12.00 p.m.	Reception for delegates and speakers — Redpath Hall

Saturday — October 8   PANEL DISCUSSIONS — Leacock Auditorium

9.30 a.m. - 11.30 a.m.	**The Development of the Caribbean Society** M. G. Smith, Lambros Comitas, James Millette, C. L. R. James
11.30 - 12.30	Lunch
12.45 p.m. - 2.30 p.m.	**The Caribbean Personality** Eduardo Seda-Bonilla, George Lamming, Robert Hill
2.30 p.m. - 3.00 p.m.	Coffee Break
3.00 p.m. - 5.00 p.m.	**The Challenge of Social Change to the Caribbean Society** Lloyd Best, M. G. Smith, Norman Girvan, Dalton Davis
5.00 p.m. - 6.00 p.m.	General Discussion
9.00 p.m.	Dance — Carpenter's Hall 3560 St. Lawrence Blvd.

C.L.R. James

James had returned to England from Trinidad about 1962, 1963, and came back to the Caribbean in 1965 to cover one of the Test cricket series in Trinidad and Tobago. His visit to Trinidad coincided with worker unrest in the country and we received news that he had been put under house arrest by Williams. James had written *Party Politics in the West Indies*, after he broke with Williams, in which, among other things, he alluded to Williams being "the ass in the lion's skin". I think that Williams probably didn't take too kindly to allusions of that nature and, using the whole coincidence of James coming to Trinidad at the time of worker unrest in the country, put the country under a state of emergency and had James put under house arrest.

Following that, James decided to plunge himself into the political arena and, having gone back to England, returned to Trinidad and Tobago and proceeded to organize the Workers' and Farmers' Party to contest the 1966 elections. I think James wanted to make a point that somebody needed to oppose Williams and bring forward a program and policy to the country. I think James' initiative was also

C.L.R. James at the home of Alfie & Pat Roberts, 1966

precipitated by what Williams had done. I feel so. In addition to being stung into that type of reaction, I still think that James must have thought that a man of his political leanings—not only leanings but his whole approach to things, his politics—would have to enter into the political arena in a very practical and concrete way in order to bring about a new day in Trinidad and Tobago. It was during that period, in preparation of that election—the whole election campaign was already underway—that we brought James in. But he didn't stay very long because after the October 1966 conference (we were holding these conferences in the Fall, in October, just after school reopened) he had to go back to campaign.

We were questioning a lot of developments in the world, and governments, whether in the Caribbean or in Africa, and we had an interest in what was happening in the socialist camp as well. So we had very open and inquiring minds about what was happening and James' intervention with us, at that point in time, was very crucial in helping us to clarify, even instinctively I think, things that we were thinking about. We got hold of a lot of his writings from the 1940s when he was in the United States and we began to read them, however superficially at times. They had a tremendous impact on us.

We discussed a lot. We used to live at 6737 De Maisonneuve Street, Apartment #2. Ann Cools had an apartment there and eventually, I think, after Ann left, Tim and Franklyn took over that place and they used to live there. I had left Carleton in the spring of 1966 and I then thought I had to go to work because I had no funds. I was even beginning to wonder if I knew how to work, too. After having gone to school for a while, you wondered if you could do anything. So I started to look for a job. I worked the first summer in the United States (1963) in a factory—Admiralty Plastics. I had a very open mind to that because it gave me an experience of working. I worked on the factory floor at the heart of industry and that dovetailed with a lot of stuff I started to read. In 1964 I worked here in Montreal in an electroplating factory in Verdun. And then I got a job in an office of a marketing survey firm and I worked there for two years. When that came to an end in 1965, I put out applications and just waited. So between the end of August, early September 1966, and the end of January 1967, I was just waiting for a job.[53] I was

[53] Roberts eventually began working for Sidbec-Dosco, a crown corporation which came into being in the early sixties when the Quebec government decided to establish an integrated steel industry. Sidbec took control of Montreal installations of Dosco, a British company.

unemployed but it gave me some time to be able to read *Capital*,[54] for example, and between that period and the time I started to work, I virtually read the whole first volume. A lot of things became much clearer to me after reading that volume and then reading a lot of other stuff. But it also allotted me time. I was in constant communication with people like Franklyn and Tim and there would be endless exchanges on different questions. If you were not sure you ran home to your books and checked. So we never really adopted any dogmatic positions. Once I figured I wasn't sure I ran to my books and then came back and said "so and so and so". We were practicing that type of open, democratic way of conversing and doing things.

James was a great influence because of the way he conducted the classes with us. We brought him back on a lecture tour of Canada and when he came here on the tour we had a lot of study sessions with him.[55]

When James was going to do something with us, even if it was just three, four of us, he took his watch out, put his watch down, and proceeded to say what he had to say as if he was talking to 300 people. And that made an impact upon us in the sense that you tend

---

[54] Karl Marx, *Capital: A Critique of Political Economy*, Volume I (1867; Moscow: Progress Publishers, 1957).

[55] Based in Montreal and Toronto between December 7, 1966 and March 8, 1967, James conducted several study group classes with the Conference Committee and gave a total of 24 public lectures in Canada and the United States. According to Robert Hill in an unpublished 1967 discussion amongst members of the Conference Committee, "there has never been a lecture [tour] so wide in scope [as] this tour by James." In addition to a number of informal talks with Caribbean groups, private groups, and small gatherings, James had engagements, in Montreal, with McGill West Indian Students' Society; a seminar for the New World Associates; meetings with The Negro Citizenship Association, the Trinidad and Tobago Association; and the St. Vincent Cricket Club; Universal Negro Improvement Association; the Centre for Developing-Area Studies, McGill University; the St. Vincent Association; and Sir George Williams University. James also spoke at the University of Windsor (Ontario); Central United Church, Detroit; and Michigan State University. In Toronto he spoke at the West Indian Students' Association (250 people attended this lecture, the largest ever at the International Students' Centre at that time), the African Students' Union, the Jamaica Canadian Association, and appeared on a special Tuesday Night Literary Program on the Canadian Broadcasting Corporation. Other engagements included Queens University's West Indian Students' Association, Kingston (Ontario) and the West Indian Students' Association, Ottawa (Ontario). James spoke on such diverse topics as the relevance of Marxism, the Russian Revolution, Caribbean politics, Shakespeare's King Lear, cricket, and George Padmore and African independence. Moreover, for James, on the heels of his Workers' and Farmers' Party defeat to Eric William's PNM in the 1966 elections in Trinidad, his presence in Montreal not only made a profound contribution to the Conference Committee's efforts, but introduced him to a whole new generation of West Indians and North Americans who barely knew of his existence, providing him with an enthusiastic audience for his ideas. It was as a result of the CCWIA activities in Montreal that James was eventually permitted to re-enter the United States for the first time since his expulsion in 1953. James returned to Montreal for the Congress of Black Writers in October 1968 and on several other occasions between 1968 and the early seventies.

to think: what importance could just a small group of people sitting down in a room have? But when we saw James, with the tradition he was coming out of and what he was involved in, that had a major impact upon us. We just devoured a lot of the stuff that he and the other people in the group that he was associated with in the 1940s produced. We devoured that information and whatever information we got our hands on.

Eventually we started to embark on other activities and we cultivated other relations in Montreal outside of ourselves. You need to have contact with people because it is only by interacting with a wider group of people that you get to understand humanity in a more comprehensive sense and make assessments about, much more profoundly than if you didn't interact with people. So we consciously sought that type of extension of our activities outside the university as well.

The Congress of Black Writers

By 1967 we organized "The West Indian Nation in Exile" because, after a while, what we were all saying is that we wanted to hold a congress in the Caribbean. That was always one of the major aims but the way things were developing in the Caribbean and given the kinds of attitudes and posturing of some of the governments in the area, it looked very unlikely that we could have done that. So in 1967 we held another conference about the "West Indian Nation in Exile". We wanted to be able to deal, concretely, with the situation of Black people here. Hence the title, "The West Indian Nation in Exile", with Orlando Patterson, Austin Clarke, and Richard B. Moore.[56] There was another fellow from the United States too, I think of Jamaican origin. I can't remember his name but we had that congress here.

I think it would be useful to say at this point that all of these congresses could be considered as a Black complement to the ongoing Quebecois Quiet Revolution. And I think that it might have been the first time in a long while that the concerns of Black people were being raised in public fora of this nature over a long period.

The Black population was seen as living below the tracks here in

[56] According to the 1967 conference program, in addition to the Jamaican sociologist and novelist Orlando Patterson, Barbadian author and one of the founders of the African Black Brotherhood in the United States, Richard B. Moore, and Barbadian novelist Austin Clarke, other participants of the 1967 conference included Guyanese writer Jan Carew, economist Lloyd Best, Joy Johnson, Dolly Wills, Carl Taylor, Barbara Jones, William Collins, Wilfred Cartey, Canute Paris, along with Alfonso (Alfie) Roberts.

Montreal, in Little Burgundy, back-to-back with the working class area of St. Henri.[57] That is where the Black population was concentrated. When I arrived in 1962, there were a lot of Black people located in the Côte-des-Neiges area, west of Côte-des-Neiges Road. There were a lot of Black West Indians there because people were beginning to move from Little Burgundy and a kind of relocation was happening. Then this grouping—Bobby, Tim, Ann Cools, then Barry Burgher would eventually join us—this developing group of people, we were now doing our thing in advance of what the *New World* group of people who were based at McGill were doing. And when we put on the Congress in 1966 there was a concern as to who we were; and, as a matter of fact, it was being asked: "who are these Reds?", especially when we brought James here. But eventually, some of those people, coming off of the McGill campus (Clary Bayne[58] was one), they now wanted to get involved with this Conference Committee. And we who had been discussing many things and attempting to cultivate a certain democratic instinct, we were being very flexible and open to other people becoming a part of this Conference Committee on West Indian Affairs and the 1967 conference ended up in a gray kind of circumstance and certain other things began to happen.[59] Wally Look-Lai had come from England and Raymond Watts arrived on the scene and a wider group of people got into organizing the Congress.[60]

[57] The adjoining working class neighbourhoods of Little Burgundy and St. Henri are located in the Southwest district of Montreal. For years, the bulk of Montreal's Black community was centred in this region, along with its core community organizations: The Negro Community Centre, Union United Church, The Coloured Women's Club, and The Universal Negro Improvement Association. In addition to its vibrant Black community, this district was also an important stop on the North American jazz circuit. Beginning in the late 1950s, the community of Little Burgundy was gentrified and, in the process, transformed into one of Canada's largest public housing projects. The Black community dispersed to other parts of Montreal while the Black population grew, largely as a result of immigration from the Caribbean. In time, Little Burgundy has developed many of the same social and economic problems that have historically plagued such public housing developments.

[58] Clarence Bayne also taught at Sir George Williams University in the sixties and later became chairman of the National Black Coalition of Canada. He is also a founding member of the Montreal-based Black Theatre Workshop and the Black Study Centre.

[59] It is not entirely clear what "gray circumstance" refers to. What has been suggested is that the core members ceded the committee to individuals who emerged in 1967 and that these "new forces" were largely inspired by the Black Power movement that was sweeping across North America. Accordingly, the new members carried the work of the committee in a more Black Nationalist direction.

[60] Prior to coming to Montreal, both Raymond Watts and Walton Look-Lai, both natives of Trinidad, were part of a study circle with C.L.R. James, Selma James, Walter Rodney, Norman Girvan, Orlando Patterson, Richard Small, Joan French and Margaret Carter Hope in England. Watts was later implicated in the protests

And given what was happening, the Conference Committee on West Indian Affairs virtually came to an end by the end of 1967. So for the 1968 Congress of Black Writers, we can't say that the Conference Committee on West Indian Affairs organized it. But the whole idea of that Congress started with us because we had wanted to have a congress in the Caribbean. As a matter of fact, Harvey and Hector had actually discussed the holding of a congress in Guyana with Burnham. There was a program and everything drawn up for that. But for some reason, I suspect it was for financial and other reasons, it never materialized.[61] So we said to ourselves we would have a congress of that nature again in Montreal.

Stokely Carmichael at the Congress of Black Writers at McGill University, Oct. 1968

The 1968 Congress was also another watershed because we know that C.L.R. James participated in it. Stokely Carmichael and James Forman of the Student Non-Violent Coordinating Committee (SNCC) in the United States came (Forman was looked upon as an ideologue) as did Harry Edwards, who was with the US Olympic team in Mexico when that demonstration of the black glove happened with Carlos.[62]

that almost toppled the government of Eric Williams in 1970. Upon returning to Trinidad from Montreal, Look-Lai became the editor of the *Vanguard*, official organ of the Oilfield Workers' Trade Union, and was later actively involved in the New Beginning Movement along with Franklyn Harvey and Bukka Rennie.

[61] According to the bulletin of the October 1967 "West Indian Nation in Exile" conference, not only did Tim Hector and Franklyn Harvey meet with Prime Minister Forbes Burnham, but Burnham actually agreed to host the following year's suggested conference, "The Caribbean Future in Light of the Caribbean Past" in Guyana. This was confirmed by a letter from Burnham's Permanent Secretary, dated March 17, 1967, to the Conference Committee, care of Franklyn Harvey.

[62] Roberts is referring to the iconic Black Power demonstration that took place at the 1968 Olympics in Mexico, in which medal-winning Black American sprinters John Carlos and Tommie Smith raised their clenched fists, donned with a black glove, in a Black Power salute as the U.S. national anthem played. Harry Edwards, then a sociologist who was associated with the Black Panther Party, is generally recognized as the person who encouraged if not orchestrated this demonstration.

Walter Rodney from Guyana and Bobby Hill, who had returned to Jamaica by then, came as did Richard Small from Jamaica or England at the time too. So those are the people who participated in that 1968 Congress.[63]

All of these conferences complemented the effervescence in the United States. Malcolm X was very popular at the time. His speeches and reaction to what was happening in the States assailed us on T.V. every night and day and that had a tremendous impact on people. After his death, Malcolm's influence was very, very strong. King was the other person who was paralleling Malcolm's activities but I think Malcolm's impact among a certain sector, especially that student sector, was extremely strong and many people were influenced by that.

The Congress was like a climax, in a sense, to the consciousness raising activity that we were engaged in at a very public level, starting with the conferences—1965, 1966, 1967, 1968—and a lot of other people got inspired to start to organize activities because at the end of those activities and the Concordia Affair, the National Black Coalition[64] came into being. Other people were stimulated and started to attempt to organize. It was the first time, as far as I know, that any dialogue at that public, organized level—bringing in people of the caliber of Lamming, a great Barbadian writer, James, and those kinds of people—had taken place before and therefore other people now thought that they could organize with their own contingent of people.

By 1967 there was another group of people who actually attempted to put on a conference. So a kind of pluralism was beginning to develop with a wider group of people and I think things

---

[63] Other guests at the Congress included the African-American psychiatrist Alvin Poussaint, Rocky Jones of Nova Scotia, Canada, and Richard B. Moore. Black Power advocate Michael X from England, along with Lloyd Best, and Jan Carew were also in attendance. Author Amiri Baraka (then Leroi Jones) and Black Panther leader Eldridge Cleaver were supposed to participate in the Congress but were prevented from doing so by U.S. authorities. Haitian writer René Depestre was listed in the Congress program but was also unable to attend.

[64] The National Black Coalition of Canada (NBCC) was founded in 1969. The impetus for the NBCC stemmed from a resolution adopted at the 1968 Montreal conference on "The Problems of Involvement in the Canadian Society with Special References to the Black Peoples of Canada". A committee was struck to follow up on the resolution and the foundation was laid for the NBCC to begin the following year. Dr. Howard McCurdy was the NBCC's first chairman. Clarence Bayne of Montreal also served as chairman. For more on the founding of the NBCC see Leo W. Bertley, *Canada and its People of African Descent* (Pierrefonds: Bilongo Publishers, 1977).

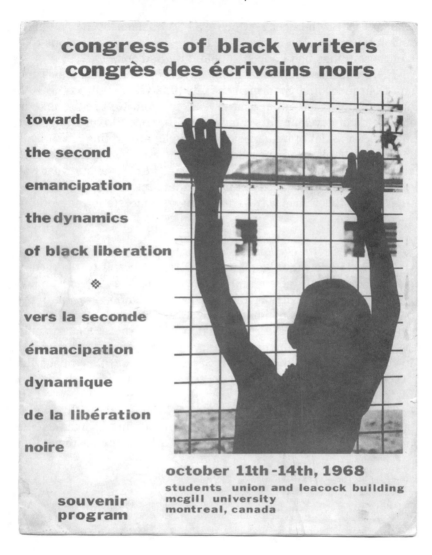

took off from there. However, we didn't think that we were doing anything astonishing and we were very conscious of the fact that we were not starting anything new and that we were just continuing what others had done before. The Negro Community Centre had been in operation here since 1928 and we were also conscious of the fact that Marcus Garvey had been here and there was a union, the

Sleeping Car Brotherhood,[65] which was an offshoot of the A. Phillip Randolph Brotherhood in the United States. We were conscious that all of those things had happened before we had come.

There was also a lot of jazz in the city. People like Miles Davis and John Coltrane would perform in the city (this year, 1995, is the 40th anniversary of the death of Charlie Parker[66]) and we used to take in those kinds of developments. So we were just open to anything, very much open to a lot of influences and flexible, attempting to cultivate the spirit, habit, and practice of democratic interchange and deliberation. We made a tremendous effort to be clear about what was happening and we just lived our lives in that kind of instinctive way— but also in a theoretical way—attempting to understand the world in which we lived.

Trouble at Sir George Williams

In 1968, some students at Concordia University charged a professor there with racism and incompetence. The charge was laid in April 1968, virtually at the end of the school year and the administration, not responding positively and properly, thought they would sweep it under the rug and hoped that the students would forget everything over the long vacation. But as soon as the students returned to school in the autumn, September 1968, they raised the question of their appeal that was not dealt with properly by the university authorities.

The Congress of Black Writers was held in October 1968 and it stimulated people further in terms of how they perceived the university's reaction.[67] Students went past a lot of the positions that

---

[65] Porters of the Canadian Pacific Railway, one of the largest employers of Blacks in Canada, became members of the International Brotherhood of Sleeping Car Porters in 1942. Black porters were often exploited and mistreated. According to Montreal author Dorothy Williams, "The signing of the contract with the CPR created a new work environment. Salaries jumped and overtime was recognized and paid. Porters enjoyed shorter work hours, an agreed grievance procedure and a greater measure of self-respect" (*The Road to Now: A History of Blacks in Montreal* [Montreal: Véhicule Press, 1997], p. 89).

[66] The year that Roberts is referring to is 1995.

[67] "The Hemispheric Conference to End the Vietnam War" was held in Montreal at the end of November and it also had an impact on the Black and Caribbean students at Sir George. According to Dennis Forsythe, the conference was attended by 2000 people and brought together "White radicals, the Black Panthers (Bobby Seale participated in the conference), Quebecois, Colombian revolutionaries, Third World fighters, Puertoricanos, Mexican student leaders, Chilean Progressives, and Canadian Pacifists. This conference reiterated many of the points of the Black Writers Congress . . ." (Forsythe, *op cit.*, p. 68).

were taken up by past students. Whereas a lot of students were dissatisfied with a lot of things that were happening at the university but kept quiet, this group of students spoke out. And in speaking out and actually going about things in a more upright and forthright manner, they also found the university authorities to be lacking in a certain amount of ethics. For example, if they went to see a professor they would be told by the secretary that the professor was not there. But once they ignored the secretary, pushed the door open, and went past the secretary, there was the professor.

So I think there were happenings like those that really instigated a lot of moral outrage by the students because a lot of us came here with a certain conception of a university; that a university is a place where you come to acquire education—education for education's sake. We didn't expect a professor to be reading notes. We expected a professor to be lecturing off the top of his head. These are some of the conceptions some of us had and those conceptions were quickly abused when we came here. Some of the professors had difficulty in putting their courses under control. I myself witnessed that a professor didn't have his course under control in an "Introduction to Political Science" class that I took in 1962. The professor had this ring binder from which he read notes and inside the ring binder he would have this book by Harold Laswell, *Who Gets What, When, How—How, When and Why*, or whatever it is,[68] reading from it too!

In those days, many of the students who had come from the Caribbean were students who had already begun to work. We were not coming here straight out of some school in the Caribbean or elsewhere like a lot of the students who we see today. We were already working, I was already managing a Customs warehouse. Some of the people who made the complaints were already working with the government and working in medical labs in the Caribbean, so that when they went to the class they could see through the assistant who was unable to differentiate between serum and plasma when working in the lab. Most of the people who made the complaint against Professor Anderson of the Biology Department of Concordia University, then Sir George Williams, were on the road to medicine. They left the Caribbean to study here and go on to medicine. So they were not just spring chickens and they were able to make their own assessments.

---

[68] Harold Laswell, *Politics: Who Gets, What, When, How?* (Cleveland and New York: Meridian Books, 1964).

Furthermore, there seems to have been a tradition that had developed in this particular course (I think it was a course in immunology that they claimed to be a fairly vital course for medicine) that the Black students invariably could get no higher than a C. I can attest to the fact that, in a course on "Political Parties" given by a man called Herbert Quinn, who was apparently one of the first products of Sir George Williams University, some of the guys who had taken the course said that no Black person could get higher than a C. And I know that happened to me because I did a course in political parties with him. We had a mid mid-term in November and I got an A; we did a mid-term, I got an A; I did a mid mid-term in about February, got an A; I did a paper, got an A and in the final I could only get a C! So that kind of thing was happening. I experienced that myself so when the events unfolded at Concordia I wasn't surprised. Other people would talk about different incidents but what everybody would say was, "Let us get through this thing in peace so that we can get on with our lives rather than causing any problems." But it so happened that with the type of atmosphere that existed, this group of students said, "No, we're not going to accept what is happening," and they decided to do something about it.

By that time I was already out of the university. I started to work in February 1967 but I kept very close to the university students. I was virtually on the inside of what was happening and knew how the students were feeling about things. And the place was in a state of effervescence, stimulated, I would say, by the Congress of Black Writers. Later on there was this African Affairs meeting[69] that was held here in the Queen Elizabeth Hotel or some place. And that conference was occupied by a lot of the students who were involved in the Sir George Affair. Kennedy Fredrick (Omowale) was involved in the occupation of the African Studies Association meeting. He came

[69] The 1969 Joint Annual Meeting on African Studies sponsored by the African Studies Association of the United States and the Committee on African Studies in Canada. In a brief admonishment printed on page three of the October 14, 1969 edition *UHURU*, one of Montreal's Black community newspapers of the time, the occupation of that meeting was presaged: "Although the word 'African' occurs throughout this announcement, these two associations are not composed of people who relate to Africans wherever they may be or to the study of them.... It is high time that black people stop these 'black experts' from setting up forums from which they try to be authorities on black people. These 'black experts' live in their white suburbs on grants given them for black studies." The occupation of that meeting by Black students, the defection of a number of Black scholars and their eventual departure from the U.S.-based African Studies Association, are seen as a defining moment in the history of African Studies in North America (Ali A. Mazrui, ed., *A General History of Africa, Vol. VIII, Africa Since 1935* [Oxford: James Curry Ltd., Berkeley: University of California Press; 1993 and 1999], pp. 715-716).

out of Petite Martinique, a dependency of Grenada. I think Leroy Butcher[70] was part of that. Rosie might have been involved in it as well. There was also a fellow by the name of Kelvin Robinson who went by the other name of Rap Brown. They used to call him Rap (there was also Rap Brown who had emerged on the scene in the United States). This Rap, Kelvin Robinson, was a very strident individual on the question with White people. There was also another fellow with Rap, Hugo Ford from Trinidad and Tobago. You had a nucleus of these guys who were very adamant.

To me, Kennedy Fredrick was a fellow finding himself as well, and there is nothing like when you just discover a "truth" and he, I think, was just finding himself and was very much influenced by Malcolm, so he was very, very outspoken and willing to go and talk to people face to face about certain things. Here were these White scholars who were saying that they were dealing with African Studies and to some of the leading students in this whole thing, they didn't think that that was the province of Whites. To demonstrate their whole opposition to that, they just took over the whole congress. They were saying: "How are these White people having a conference of African people?" The same thing happened at the Congress of Black Writers where they said that Black people have to caucus, must be able to deliberate by themselves. And it was said that the presence of White people always had a disruptive impact and therefore Black people should do things by themselves.

The Sir George Williams thing began in 1968 and that whole agitation would continue on the campus into February 1969 when the decision was taken to occupy the Computer Centre, lasting another two weeks. It was a tremendous historical occurrence, a social thunderclap because it announced, loud and clear to the whole society, that Black people were here. I'm talking about February 11, 1969, when the smoke started to emerge from the ninth story of the Sir George Hall Building and there was a tremendous crowd of people, hundreds of people, gathered in the area. It announced loud and clear that Black people were here, and not only below the tracks, but inside the whole society. It had that kind of effect. And all of this coincided with tremendous worker unrest here because the working

---

[70] Leroy Butcher of St. Lucia was one of the occupants during the Sir George Williams Affair and later became the director of the Côte-des-Neiges Project, one of several community organizations that emerged in Montreal's Black community in the wake of the incident.

class, or the trade unions, were out in the streets—the CSN, the QFL[71] led by Laberge, and there was another union I think led by a man called Marcel Pepin. Pepin, Laberge, and a fellow called Yvon Charbonneau—those are the three guys who were uniting in pursuing their union objectives here.[72] So while all of that was happening, we were carrying on our activities, all of which were complementary to those.

Lessons from an Occupation

By February 11, the occupation was at least two weeks old. There was a hearing committee established with certain points set out in terms of what the students wanted. But that hearing committee was aborted because one of the members of the committee was said to have been of South African origin and once that was known the students said they didn't want any part of that. In addition, there were one or two other Black people who I think the students were suspect of.[73] So that hearing committee broke up. It never got anywhere.

In one of the regular meetings that were being held in some of the university classrooms, a Haitian by the name of Phillipe Filsaimé[74] was the first person that I heard make the point about occupying the Computer Centre. There were also people like Kennedy Fredrick,[75]

---

[72] Louis Laberge became president of the QFL in 1964; Marcel Pepin became president of the CSN in 1965; and Yvon Charbonneau became the president of the Corporation des enseignants du Québec. Michel Chartrand was another leading figure in the labour movement during the sixties. Chartrand became president of the Parti Socialiste du Québec (PSQ) in 1963, the year it was founded. Its provisional council was comprised almost exclusively of trade unionists from the QFL and the CSN. Chartrand would later become the leader of the CSN's Montreal Central Council. For more information on Quebec's labour history see Anon., *A History of the Labour Movement in Quebec* (Montreal and New York: Black Rose Books, 1987).

[73] Chester Davis of the United States and Clarence Bayne were the two Black Sir George professors who the students opposed having on the hearing committee after meeting with them, feeling they were perhaps incapable of judging the case with impartiality.

[74] Phillipe Filsaimé was one of the leading actors in the Sir George Williams Affair and one of the accused after the students were arrested on February 11, 1969. Filsaimé gained notoriety during the trial of the students for presenting the prosecutor with a "gift" box which contained a homemade "voodoo doll" garbed in a black robe, white stock, and with a pierced heart with a bloody mark. Filsaimé's "gift" created quite a stir, and even a scare, in the courtroom. Filsaimé is also the author of *Cajénol: Tranches de vie d'un nouveau venu à Montréal* (Montreal: Grafik Universel: Editions, n.d.).

[75] Kennedy Fredrick (Omowale) is a native of Petite Martinique, Grenada. He was one of the most militant and vociferous of the agitators during the Sir George Williams Affair. Facing potential imprisonment (as were Rosie Douglas and Ann Cools), Omowale left Canada and eventually moved to Tanzania with his wife, Viola

Kelvin Robinson, Leroy Butcher from St. Lucia, Bukka Rennie[76]—Who else? The Stephens, coming out of Dominica, Rosie Douglas and Ann Cools, originally of Barbados. She's your first Black Canadian woman senator. There was Brenda Dash, a Black American girl,[77] Franklyn James, from St. Lucia and a fellow called Hilary, a St. Lucian. He was going to school in the United States but Vietnam was in the air and in order to avoid going to Vietnam he came here and was going to school. There were three young men coming out of St. Vincent and the Grenadines who got caught up in Sir George. A fellow called Wantumi Thomas, whose father was chief of police in St. Vincent and the Grenadines. There was Hubert Prescod and Ronald Ambrose and another guy from St. Vincent called Rodney John. He is now a Ph.D. psychologist. There was another fellow called "Jughead,"[78] a Jamaican in medicine: he's a doctor today. There was also Linette's sister.[79] She is now a lawyer. A lot of people that were involved in the Sir George Williams Affair completed their degrees and went on to become professional people.[80]

Now, we must remember what was taking place internationally. There were student struggles virtually almost everywhere in this

(Aduke) Daniel, joining Walter and Patricia Rodney. Omowale met Walter Rodney in 1968 during the Congress of Black Writers.

[76] One of the organizers of the Congress of Black Writers, Bukka Rennie, later became a leading member of the New Beginning Movement along with Franklyn Harvey in Trinidad. Rennie is the author of *The history of the working-class in the 20th century (1919-1956): the Trinidad and Tobago experience* (Toronto: New Beginning Movement, 1973), and *Revolution and Social Development: A Direct Address to the Unemployeds of Trinidad and Tobago* (Trinidad and Tobago: New Beginning, 1975).

[77] Brenda Dash was of African Canadian descent.

[78] "Jughead" was the nickname of Douglas Mossop, one of the original complainants in the Sir George Williams dispute.

[79] Roberts is referring to Linette Edwards of Trinidad, a long-standing community worker in the Montreal Black community and a close friend and associate of Alfie Roberts. The sister that he refers to is Glenda Edwards.

[80] Other students included Allan Brown, later a member of the International Caribbean Service Bureau, Cheddi Jagan, the son of the late prime minister of Guyana, and Coralee Hutchinson. According to Rosie Douglas, Hutchinson was a casualty of police brutality during the Sir George protests. In an unpublished October 17, 2000 interview, Douglas says that Hutchinson of the Bahamas received a hard blow to her skull from the butt of a police officer's baton when she was arrested on February 11, 1969, after responding to a racist remark by the officer. She later began to suffer from headaches and died of a brain tumor about a year after. For a more complete list of the students that were involved or accused of being actively involved in the Sir George Williams Affair (Eber, *op. cit*, p. 318).

Western World. There was what was happening in France in 1968 with the student movement led by a fellow named Cohn-Bendit who was of German origin—Rudy the Red, as they eventually started to call him—and that whole big thing shook France.[81] What took place in France was also very important for us because I think it confirmed what James was talking about; here it was that in an advanced Western country, wherein people say that the proletariat was bought out and was consumer-oriented, that a general strike brought the whole of France to a standstill. De Gaulle virtually fled and left for Germany! All that was needed was for some force to tip it over. And there was what was happening in student circles in the United States.[82] It was a very heady period. In Czechoslovakia, there was another movement underway, coming from within the Communist Party of Czechoslovakia, introducing what they called "socialism with a human face."[83]

So we had these things happening all over the world. You had a lot of activities going on in the Caribbean too. I think people were also out in Aruba at the time.

[81] The May 1968 mass protest in France shook the country to its foundation and almost toppled the DeGaulle regime. Daniel Cohn-Bendit, a student, played a leading role in the early stages of the demonstrations. For an analysis of France, May 1968 from the perspective of a former member of the Conference Committee on West Indian Affairs, see Franklyn Harvey in *Caribbean International Opinion: Dynamics of Liberation* (October 1968), published by the Publishing Committee of the Caribbean Nation, an outgrowth of the Conference Committee, based in Montreal. In addition to Harvey's brief but poignant essay, this historic publication includes contributions from Arnim Eustace, former prime minister of St. Vincent and the Grenadines, Rosie Douglas, Alfie Roberts, Tim Hector and C.L.R. James.

[82] In the late sixties and early seventies, university campuses all over North America were the sites of heated, often bloody protests between students (and professors at times) struggling for more open and democratic practices within the university. In Montreal, for example, Students for a Democratic University and student leader and lecturer Stanley Gray held sit-ins and mass demonstrations in the late sixties on the McGill University Campus. In 1968, protests and occupations organized by Students for a Democratic Society at Columbia University, New York and in Chicago were met with bloody repression by the police and received international media coverage (Tim and Julyan Reid, eds., *Student Power and the Canadian Campus* [Toronto: Peter Martin Associates Limited, 1969] and Walt Anderson, ed., *The Age of Protest* [Pacific Palisades: Goodyear Publishing Company Inc., 1969]). Black student protests, particularly in the United States, also contributed to the founding of a number of Black Studies programs and courses throughout North America, including at Sir George Williams University (Forsythe, *op. cit.*, and Armstead L. Robinson, Craig C. Foster, and Donald H. Ogilvie, *Black Studies in the University Setting* [New Haven: Yale University Press, 1969]).

[83] In the spring of 1968, known as the "Prague Spring", major social reforms were undertaken by the Communist Party of Czechoslovakia as a new, more moderate leadership replaced the old. Past economic and social policies were criticized and new political freedoms were encouraged. Czechoslovakia also experienced an explosion in film, music, and culture generally. Criticism of the reforms in the Soviet Bloc began to surface, culminating in the August 20-21, 1968, Soviet invasion of Czechoslovakia and the beginning a twenty year period of "normalization".

The Sir George Williams occupation taught some of us another thing. I was breaking my head over this question of organization and that incident taught me more than anything I could have ever read anywhere. I think it confirmed what James was always attempting to say on the whole question of submission to authority. The day that the occupation took place, I came straight to the university from work. Given the relationship that we had with some of the students, Viola Daniel, now known as Aduke (she got married eventually to Kennedy Fredrick in Tanzania) and I were put in charge of the door.[84] Every single person simply accepted our authority at the door. People fished inside of their pockets saying, "This is my I.D.," professors and everybody. So that exposed something to us. Secondly, in the occupation in the Computer Centre, the computers themselves were kept at a certain temperature in a certain sector of the room and the students who did the occupying allocated people to deal with all of that. It seemed to me that people just fell automatically into certain positions, confirming what I think James was attempting to say in most of his writings. Nobody organized it. (At least that is what I think because I was not part of the inner group in terms of that.) People just fell in place.

Even going back to the Bolshevik Revolution in October 1917, the most educated government in Europe, where you had highly educated people—as James would say and a lot of people would admit—considering the roles that they carried out after the October Revolution (like in the Civil War), people who were highly educated turned out to be political commissars in the military sphere. So some of us who were thinking in certain ways saw in front of our very eyes a lot of things we were thinking about manifested in practice. What was happening with this whole academic business was that you came to school to study economics. And most people seemed to be thinking, "Well I'm heading for a job in economics." Or you came and studied some other discipline in order to get a job in that discipline. But many of us never thought like that. We never thought it would happen that way. For us, you came and you studied and you never knew what would happen. In my own sphere, I did a major in Public Administration and Political Economy and, based on my qualifications, I don't think I would necessarily get a job in that area. So what I'm saying is that individuals have other qualities than what

[84] The door to the computer room where the occupation was taking place.

they are supposed to be educated in. What people do is stereotype you; you have a degree in Political Science so you should know about politics. People had a stereotype about an engineer or scientist, that somehow he's apolitical. With our group here with us we found that some of the most political people were the people in those disciplines. Take someone like Franklyn. Franklyn was an engineer. And we began to meet other people like that. So there were a lot of things that we were thinking that we saw happen in practice, and confirming in many ways some of the ideas that we instinctively held.

I had a very good rapport with the students. I was the person who drew up the conditions for the hearing committee for the students. I think it was about a four-point thing. Even at one point (was it after they were freed or before?) we put out an issue one night and I was put in charge of seeing the issue out. That was put out on a cyclostyle thing (I don't think I even have a copy of that) called *This is Your University*. And then after that I was also one of the people who helped prepare the special issue of *The Georgian*. The White students who were in charge of *The Georgian* turned it over to us and we put out what was called *The Black Georgian*.

One of the questions that I saw very early during the occupation was that you were a sitting duck, because you occupied the building and you're just there. And I remember myself turning to somebody and telling them that the police could come in any minute. So I was always very conscious of the limitations of an occupation. (I can't remember if it was around that time in Latin America in particular where a lot of kidnapping was taking place. The Tupamaros[85] were kidnapping a lot of people and that eventually had an influence here in Quebec where the FLQ abducted Cross, who was the English Commissioner or English diplomat here. So you kidnap a guy and rush into a house and after that where do you go from there? You have no movement with whom you're affiliated to do anything else and you just rush in the house and hope until you get fed-up and you surrender or somebody finds you.) Given our own analysis in terms of how we thought certain struggles should be pursued, we saw the limitations of an occupation. But the occupation made a point though, you must understand. However, what we were seeing was that the occupation had no relation to any other movement. We were

85 The Tupamaro National Liberation Movement was an urban guerilla movement based in Uruguay that made international headlines when they kidnapped Geoffrey Jackson, the British Ambassador to Uruguay (*The Tupamaros* [London: Secker and Warburg, 1972]).

concerned that you were just a sitting duck in there. And that would happen in the Sir George occupation. If the police had gone in some other night they would have arrested a completely different set of people. They might have held a certain core but they could have also held a lot of different people because people would cook food and carry it for the occupiers and just sit in there. So we were always conscious of all of that.

One night I actually told my people in my house that I'll be home by eleven o'clock. I would go to the occupation every evening from work and not get home until two, three o'clock in the morning. I would be up by six, having to go to work. I said that I was going to be home by eleven o'clock but when I was just about to leave the university, about eleven, the matter had been put to a teachers association at the university and the verdict that came back was negative. I couldn't leave in those circumstances. I had to hang around because in a situation like that, if you're thinking a certain way, you don't leave. But anyway, by about 2:30 that morning I decided to leave. But funny, when I was leaving I saw a man called Magnus Flynn and his assistant coming in with some other people. And I said to myself, "that looks funny." And no sooner had I put my head on my pillow, by about six o'clock, I received a call at home telling me that the police were in the building.

So I moved right away. There was a group of students staying over on Mackay. At nights, Carl Paris, a Barbadian—I think he now teaches at the University of the West Indies—he and I would prepare communiqués from within the occupation. We organized a demonstration around the building for the occupants.[86] Hundreds of people came. I had wider contacts than some of those students so I called Mergler right away. Mergler was a lawyer, a progressive lawyer whom we had all heard about and knew. So I called Mergler and talked to him about what was happening and he was willing to take up the case right away.[87]

In those days you had the Eastern Caribbean Commission down

[86] While supporters of the occupants demonstrated in front of Sir George Williams building, some students and other onlookers chanted "Let the Niggers Burn!" as they watched the smoke filter out of the computer room on the ninth floor of the Hall Building where the students were trapped in a fire. Of the 97 students who were arrested, 42 were Black and there were 30 women. Upon arrest, the occupants were separated according to color: Whites went to one cell and Blacks were sent to another.

[87] Bernard Mergler represented Kennedy Fredrick, Rosie Douglas, Phillipe Filsaimé, among other defendants, in the case against the students of the Sir George Williams Affair. His associate attorneys were

in Place Bonaventure. It was then headed by a man called Novelle Richards from Antigua and Barbuda, an old labour leader with Vere Bird from Antigua. We went there and asked him if he could use his diplomatic initiative or his diplomatic position to get in touch with the University administration and see what he could do. He said he couldn't do much and basically that petered out. But there was another demonstration of something that hasn't been seen here since. We don't know where they came from but Black people lined up to go into that apartment on Mackay where Carl Paris was living to make their contribution to a fund. I think that was another manifestation of what James was projecting in terms of what masses of people can do on certain occasions. People just lined up in silence to make their contributions.

After that, we set up the February 11th Defense Committee to raise funds for the case. That activity took us quite into the seventies. It was then that the UNIA Liberty Hall would come into wider knowledge.[88] Leon Jacobs, now a professor over at Dawson College, and a fellow by the name of Norman Cook, another Black American, went to a man called Mr. Tucker,[89] now deceased, who was in charge of the Garvey-UNIA administration and asked for the use of the hall. He agreed to let us use the hall and every Thursday night there was a meeting there. A man called Roy States (also deceased) who was like an in-house lecturer on the history of Black people and he used to give lectures at the hall and communion used to take place there.

So all of that was happening and people's consciousness was lifted and a lot of people became more sensitized. Apart from listening to Malcolm X and listening to what was going on in the United States, this was happening right here in Montreal.

Pierre Lacaille and his assistant, Juanita Westmoreland, a young up-and-coming Black lawyer. Today, Juanita Westmoreland is Quebec's first Black Supreme Court judge.

[88] The Universal Negro Improvement Association, founded by Marcus Garvey of Jamaica in 1914 became the largest Black mass movement the world has seen. By 1928 there were 996 chapters of the UNIA around the world, 725 of which were in the United States. The Montreal chapter (Division Five) of the UNIA was established on June 9, 1919, and is one of the oldest existing chapters remaining.

[89] Ellis J. Tucker was president of the Montreal Chapter of the UNIA from 1935 to 1975 and a tireless community worker within the Montreal Black community. A subsequent president of the UNIA, Henry Langdon, was also a relative of Louise Langdon, mother of Malcolm X. Born in Grenada, Louise Langdon moved to Montreal, Canada, where she joined her uncle Edgerton Langdon, a staunch Garveyite, and became an active organizer within the Montreal chapter of the UNIA. It was at a Montreal UNIA conference that she met Earl Little, Malcolm X's father. They eventually married in 1919.

Members of the Caribbean International Service Bureau. L-R: Viola Daniel, Barry Burgher, Alfie Roberts

Alfie Roberts (third row up, 2nd from left) in Moscow at the World Congress of Peace, 1973

Top Left: Alfie in Dar es Salaam, Tanzania as a delegate of the Sixth Pan-African Congress, 1974

Top Right: Alfie at work at Sidbec-Desco Steel

Bottom Left: Alfie at home in Montreal

Alfie in Ghana, 1983

Alfie and Pat Roberts with Senator Ann Cools (centre) in Ottawa, 1995

Afterword

Alfie . . . speak his name in any part of the Black community of Montreal and people instantly recognize without further description of whom you speak. For there was only one Alfie and no one can or will ever take his place in the esteem and affection of the Black Montreal community. The whole community was his parish; at any hour of the night one might call him and he would be seemingly awake, ready to respond to any request for help or advice or just to talk.

Speak his name and there are those who will remember Alfie travelling the streets of Montreal on foot, which was his preference. Stopping to talk with Alfie would often evolve into a virtual seminar. The street was as much a classroom for Alfie as was the university campus. Most importantly, Alfie always had time for everyone, he never made anyone feel like he was rushing on his way to get some place. He not only made time for everyone, but he also learned from them and shared with them what he knew.

Reading his memoir of those early days in Montreal I now see that Alfie brought with him the pedagogy of the Customs warehouse in St. Vincent that he had worked in as a young man. Indeed, it was there that, as Alfie recalls it, he found himself completely confounded by a question that was put to him. What has to be grasped is that the Customs warehouse happened to be not only the official warehouse in the country; it was also the site of a special kind of Caribbean sociality—a place where it was customary for work and ideas to mingle. Alfie was nurtured in this atmosphere of rational freethinkers, Caribbean freethinkers who were always accustomed to think through the basis of their beliefs. It was this powerful commitment to reason that made him resolve that day to pursue a university education solely as a means of finding an answer to the question that had stumped him.

Imagine that! Considering the great expense in terms of time and resources in completing a university degree, to say nothing of the uncertainty and unfamiliarity of doing it in a foreign (and extremely cold) country, where one was daily confronted with the racism of the society and its institutions—imagine putting up with all of that and feeling it was worth it, if, in the end, it led him to finding the answer he sought.

If the question was the thing that propelled him, however, in his pursuit of the answer he re-created and replicated in Montreal the same inquiring ambience of the Customs warehouse in St. Vincent—a place where the mundane work of counting and registering and releasing goods was leavened by the daily exhilaration of clerks and laborers interrogating their colonized life-world. In this sense, Alfie left St. Vincent, but St. Vincent never left Alfie. The Alfie who was so convinced that he was never going to leave St. Vincent and who could not be tempted with pleasing offers eventually made a home in Montreal for Patricia his beloved and himself and their three children. The entire Black community of Montreal became his extended family, once again affirming the tradition that Alfie brought with him from home. He was a freethinker, but it was a role that was always in the service of the Black community.

As the years progressed and the dream of returning home receded, Alfie made the Black community of Montreal his own very special province. He could not have known that within a few short years he and others would found in Montreal one of the great contemporary centers of Caribbean consciousness, in the process making Canada today one of the key cultural and political capitals of the entire Caribbean region. That was certainly not the case when Alfie first stepped forth on Canadian soil in 1962. Through Alfie and others like him, Canada has become a different country—a better country—and for this Canada owes Alfie a great and lasting debt.

I would like to go back to that question that was asked in the Customs warehouse back in St. Vincent. I remember Alfie himself describing to me the conversation in which the question was put. In outline, Alfie said that one day he and a group of men were discussing some subject having to do with Black people (which, from the sound of it, was more like every day!), when suddenly someone sallied forth. "If all you know so much about Black people," the person said, "then answer me this, how come no African ever built a motor-car?" Alfie told me that the conversation ground to a complete halt. He said he was dumbfounded by the question and could not respond. That story, like all the rest in *Alfie Speaks,* is vintage Alfie.

Now, I find myself thinking about the question and wish that Alfie could be here to discuss it further. In the background what animates the question and gives it such force is not some empirical truth but anxiety—the anxiety that the colonized is made to feel, that silences the colonized. Where does this anxiety come from? It originates, in my view, from the deliberate erasure under colonialism of the lived experience of the colonized people in question, in this instance the people of St. Vincent. The colonized are educated out of knowing anything about their own life world; instead, as the great W. E. B. Du Bois observed in *The Souls of Black Folk* (1903), things are so arranged that we end up "always looking at one's self through the eyes of others, of measuring one's soul by the tape of a world that looks on in amused contempt and pity." Contempt and pity. That was the burden that the colonized bore, was meant to bear, and the result was self-doubt that oftentimes immobilized the colonized.

It was this poisoned state of mind that Alfie set out to struggle against and by doing so to try to undo its grasp. Today one reads in the account of his striving and the travail that he endured how and why it shaped the future course of his life. In that sense, *Alfie Speaks* stands as a valuable historical document from a member of the colonized world—of how one individual sought to decolonize his mind and heal the mental and emotional wound inflicted by this blight on the mental horizon of black folk—"how come no African ever built a motor-car?"

Now, as I have myself come to ponder the question, I realize that it could only have possessed the special valency that it did, in terms of its power to disrupt and disturb, by virtue of the complete absence of information about what Black people actually *did*, without which knowledge one would not only end up bewildered but, ideologically speaking, dispossessed. This state of intellectual dispossession was disabling in its effect, a kind of general mental anaesthesia. The question, to begin with, ought never to have been seriously entertained, if, for example, that day in the Customs warehouse the audience had been aware of the story that appeared in *The Times* of London, in its issue of June 20th, 1844, viz.

A **WEST INDIAMAN.**—Considerable curiosity was excited on Tuesday at the St. Katharine's Docks in consequence of the arrival of a vessel from Bermuda of only 41 tons burden, manned entirely by men of colour, and having a cargo consisting almost entirely of arrow root, which has accomplished the voyage in the incredibly short space of 31 days. This Liliputian vessel has only one mast, her sides are not more than from 12 to 15 inches from the deck, having a hand-rail raised above them of about the same height; the stern is quite even with the deck, open and unprotected; and altogether she has more the appearance of a yacht, than a vessel capable of journeying a voyage across the Atlantic. Though so small, she is evidently of great strength, and has not a vestige of paint or ornament about her.

The month after the appearance of the *Times* report, *The Friend of the Africans* (July 1844) published the report with the following accompanying information:

We have been informed, that the above-mentioned vessel has been entirely built, manned, and equipped by emancipated Negroes—that they were the sole growers and shippers of the cargo, and that their capital alone has been embarked in the speculation. May we not reasonably hope for a wide extension of this enterprising spirit, when transplanted to the still more important land of their fathers, and look forward to docks and quays crowded with the native products and vessels belonging to the farmers and merchants of Africa? (p. 20)

The point I am trying is to make is that there was never any objective significance to the notion of an African ever having built a motor-car. What mattered, ultimately, was the meaning subjectively attached to the idea. For it to have had the force that it had for Alfie was more a reflection of the intellectual *void* in which it was presented—the complete absence of anything like a history of the Caribbean people was what allowed the people to be so easily insulted and misled and held up to such "contempt and pity," to quote Du Bois.

Moreover, I wonder how many people present that day in the Customs warehouse where Alfie was working knew anything of Capt. Hugh N. Mulzac (1886-1971), who, even though he was a Vincentian, lived in the U.S. In 1918, Mulzac became the first Black person in U.S. history to win his Master's License and who was the chief officer of Marcus Garvey's Black Star Line vessel, s. s. *Yarmouth,* on its second and third Caribbean voyages. Born on Union Island in the Grenadines, Mulzac began his career at the age of eighteen. He attended Swansea Nautical College, in Swansea, Wales, before serving as a deck officer on various British and American vessels in

World War I. He became a U. S. citizen in 1918. After he ended his service with the Black Star Line, Mulzac formed his own steamship company. In 1921 he established Mulzac's Nautical Academy, eventually enrolling fifty-two students. In 1942, following the U. S. entry into World War II, Capt. Mulzac was given the captaincy of the U. S. Navy's s.s. *Booker T. Washington*. He was inducted posthumously, in 1984, into the U. S. National Maritime Hall of Fame.

Could they have known anything of the Bishop William Benjamin Derrick (1848-1913), who came to America during the Civil War from Antigua? In 1888 he was elected secretary of the AME Church and elected bishop in 1896, a position that he held for seventeen years. As the presiding bishop of the AME New York diocese, Derrick has been described as "the most influential West Indian Republican [politician] and perhaps the most popular and respected West Indian politician in [New York] city until his death in 1913" (Calvin B. Holder, "The Rise of the West Indian Politician in New York City, 1900-1952," *Afro-Americans in New York Life and History* 4, no. 1 [January 1980]: 46).

The same question could be asked about D. Augustus Straker (1842-1908), one of America's great civil rights lawyers. After graduating from Codrington College in Barbados and becoming principal of St. Mary's Public School, Straker left Barbados for America in 1868 following the Civil War to assist in educating the former slaves. His books include *Reflections on the Life and Times of Toussaint L'Ouverture* (1885), *The New South Investigated* (1888), *A Trip to the Windward Islands* (1896), and two important legal treatises, *Circuit Court Commissioner's Guide: Law and Practice* (1897) and *Compendium of Evidence* (1899). Again, one could also cite the career achievements at the turn of the century of other outstanding West Indians, such as Rev. Joseph N. Durant, D.D., of Barbados and Rev. J. E. Rawlins of Antigua.

What should be obvious from any such review is that the wrong question was being asked and that, furthermore, it was being asked of the wrong party. The real question or questions that needed to be asked was—how and why was the history of the Caribbean people hidden and withheld and to what end? Why was the falsely abstract question of the building of the motor-car freighted with so much anxiety? How did it manage to displace far more pertinent experiences? It was never at any time a question of intelligence or competence *per se.* Behind the grotesquerie of the question stood the might and power of the colonial order which was all that, ultimately, enforced the standing of reality on its head in such a way as to confuse and manipulate the thinking of the colonized. It turns out that, all along, colonialism was a gigantic confidence game— constructed on an illusion, the illusion of the incapacity of the colonized and the so-called civilizing mission of the colonizer. It is frightening now to contemplate how much confusion and havoc this historical fraud has wrought in the minds of the colonized. The colonial pretense of civilizing the native and the 'dark continent' was what alone made meaningful and lent credence to the question that so puzzled Alfie. The flipside to this pretense, of course, was the violent brutality and savagery of imperial self-preservation whenever it was threatened. But if the question of the relationship of the African to the putative motor-car represented a dilemma that Alfie felt obliged to address, it never obscured from his view the presence of important people in his midst from whom he did learn a great deal. Alfie paid attention to everything: from the people in the Kingstown market to the news bulletins stuck up outside the "doctor shop" for passers by to read and digest. He studied people closely and was attentive to their stories and their quirks. Nothing slipped Alfie by. He carried their stories within him for the rest of his life, so much so that *Alfie Roberts Speaks* constitutes one of the keenest pieces of social and political observation of a young man coming of age in the Caribbean that exists.

The irony is that when Alfie finally arrived in Canada, not only was he well prepared intellectually; most importantly, he came fully prepared to take on the best that Canada had to offer. It was Canada that was ignorant of what it was getting in Alfie and the thousands of other West Indians who settled in Canada in the 1960s. Our very presence in Canada was a refutation that history always is the history of the strongest. Alfie's life in microcosm argues compellingly that in the long term the colonized, if they survive, are bound to have a greater impact on history than the colonizers, because it is they who demonstrate that intentions of the colonizers in history rarely coincide with what actually happens.

Here was the real life answer to that infernal question manifesting itself in concretely real terms, and not by means of a specious scholastic exercise masquerading as a serious historical argument.

What readers hold in their hands is the story of a particular individual, albeit a most remarkable man, through whose narrative we are able to track the early hope followed by subsequent disillusionment as the nationalist movements throughout the Caribbean betrayed their promise and potential. Alfie came to Canada at the time of the collapse of the aborted West Indies Federation. Surprisingly, Alfie held no bitterness in the wake of its dissolution—it was not worth saving, he tells us, for he understood that at bottom it was a colonial venture, so that its collapse was no real disaster. I remember at the time the expressions of bitterness directed against Jamaica after Jamaica voted to withdraw from the Federation. And Alfie? He says that he understood why Jamaica voted to withdraw and no one should accuse Jamaica of bad faith. This is quintessential Alfie who refrained from personalizing political tragedy and who always looked for the moral in any political defeat in order to learn and move on.

If one chapter in Alfie's life was closing and another was opening when he moved to Montreal, it was in Canada that the people of the West Indies would meet up under new circumstances. Out of this meeting a new political vision of the Caribbean would be born. Such was the power and encompassing nature of the vision that came into being on Canadian soil that Canada itself would be forced to deal with the multi-faceted nature of the Caribbean reality in its midst. The flash-point was ultimately ignited in the tragedy of the Sir George Williams University affair.

Alfie's description of what went on behind the scenes adds new insights into the background of the grievances leading up to the confrontation as well as the events surrounding the occupation of the university's Computer Room. Alfie speaks as one who was there and who knew what went on. The result is a somber, even self-critical, analysis of the difficulties that the students faced with courage and bravery. When the final story of these events come to be told, Alfie's testimony will undoubtedly form part of it. Alfie's perspective represents only that of a single individual and doubtless other participants in those tragic events would have widely varying perspectives. But this is precisely what makes Alfie's account historically so valuable.

My very first meeting with Alfie was following a lecture I had been invited to give at Sir George Williams University (I was then an undergraduate at the University of Toronto). I met him standing outside the auditorium with his friend Kerwin Morris. I walked up to him and introduced myself and that was the beginning of our friendship. The year was either 1964 or 1965—forty years ago. Our friendship would become one of the most important things in my life. Wherever in the world that I happened to be at any point in time, Alfie would somehow track me down and would call to find out how I was doing. (I confess that I would often try to limit the conversation, thinking about his phone bill, but anyone who knew Alfie knows how futile a gesture that was.) Our very last conversation was while I was on sabbatical in Swansea, Wales. Alfie was then in hospital nearing the end of his illness. I hoped that he would be alive for me to visit him one last time—alas, he passed away the very week I returned to the United States. I miss him a great deal, most of all his deep humanity.

In one of our telephone conversations Alfie said something to me that sums up who he was for me. I can't recall that it was apropos of anything in particular. He was just being Alfie, always reflecting on what moral could be found in some formative experience.

"When I was boy," he mused, "I used to wonder at the fact that when I had cleaned my room and put away all my clothes and arranged everything in its proper place, cleaned all my shoes, and everything was nice and orderly, eventually the room got to the point where it had to be cleaned again, and the whole process would start over. The clothes in my chest of drawer would never stay the way that I had arranged them. I often used to wonder about this, of always having to start over, when only days before everything was spick and span. As a boy I used to ask myself why this was, why nothing ever stayed the same. I found out that this is how life is—you always return to that which you think you have accomplished and no sooner than you are done, you start all over again."

How I wish that Alfie was here with us, in order that we might continue the conversation as one of those new beginnings that he spoke about. To cite just one example: Alfie speaks about many things in his reminiscences, yet there is one topic that he does not bring up: the Vietnam War. The liberation struggle of the Vietnamese people was a momentous event, certainly among the greatest events of the twentieth-century and one that formed a key part of our generation's political consciousness. That it does not appear in the narrative merely reflects the fact that the interview from which Alfie's reminiscences are extracted followed a particular agenda.

Today I would love to listen to Alfie reflecting on Vietnam and the significance of the war of liberation fought by the heroic Vietnamese people. Walter Rodney once confided to me that the Vietnamese "carried on their backs all of us," namely, all of the people of the Third World. I don't think that Alfie would have disagreed with this assessment, but knowing Alfie, I know that he would have been sensitive to special aspects of that struggle that we might have missed or failed to grasp the significance of, especially the human side of the struggle. And with his deep insight the struggle would become illuminated in new and unsuspected ways.

Alas, it will not be possible now. Continuing the conversation will be up to us who knew him and to those who come after. What Alfie has left us is a remarkable historical memoir to ponder and to apply to our circumstances wherever we are today. It is absolutely faithful to the person that I knew and loved. We should be very thankful for it. I would urge that we re-commit ourselves to his memory and resolve in any way that is feasible to continue his life-work, and that not the least way to do so might be through the recently launched program of *The Alfie Roberts Institute.*

Speak his name.

Robert A. Hill
Los Angeles, California
February, 2005

The Alfie Roberts Institute

The Alfie Roberts Institute is an independent education and research centre based in Montreal, Canada. One of the chief objectives of the Institute is to encourage study and research on the history and social development of communities of African and Caribbean descent. In addition to maintaining a library and documentation centre, the Institute produces publications, organizes forums and expositions, and offers courses and workshops.

For more information on the Alfie Roberts Institute call (514) 313-8938 or visit our website: www.ari-iar.org

You can also write to us at:

The Alfie Roberts Institute
5871 Victoria, Suite 220
Montreal, Quebec
H3W 2R7
Canada